Prayers
Against
Addiction

**Praying for Your Addict
Where the Needle
Pierces Skin**

S. E. Tschritter & Ashley Worrell

WITH Erin Niebuhr Hernandez,

Larry J. Leech II AND Kelly Evans

Contents

A note from
S.E. Tschritter

The Prayers You'll Find:

I craved authentic prayers about addiction, unedited pleas from both addicts and loved ones watching someone battle addiction demons. God answered my prayers and placed people on my path who each lend unique, valuable insights to battling addiction.

- A former heroin addict, **Erin's** prayers focus on other addicts she knows and praying them out of dangerous situations. When you grab your copy of *The Prodigal's Son: Crackhead to Jesus Freak*, you'll see Erin. She was my first call after my conversations with the police sergeant and the nurse. "Erin, Clint was in an accident last night. I think alcohol was involved." She said, "bring them over." End call. I chose her that morning because she'd been there, and when you've been there, you don't need explanations.
- **Ashley** is a recovering alcoholic. In her vulnerable prayers, she begs God for strength on her ongoing sobriety journey. Ashley's authenticity drew me to her. She unapologetically owns her story and follows God's unconventional path. Ashley is also braver than she realizes.
- **Larry** witnessed multiple family members battle addictions. His heart is to help others give voice to their own experiences. He wholly believes every story matters and helps others articulate what they can't put into words themselves.
- **Kelly,** my daughter, is thirteen years old and the daughter of a man who battled addiction and depression. Six years ago, after her dad died, Kelly was afraid of storms. I told her that thunder was her dad playing football in heaven, colliding with other player's helmets on the line. Now she dances in the rain.

- **Me,** the widow of an addict. We found my pastor-husband's cancer through a drunk driving accident after an alcohol relapse, a statement I'd never dreamed I'd say. As the wife of an addict, I prayed so deep into the night, I imagined only God Himself was still awake. Not beautiful, eloquent words, but blubbery cries for redemption.

Within this book, that's what you'll find—transparency, authenticity, raw emotion, and space for you to add your own desperate pleas.

The Prodigal Promise:

A great deal of thought went into naming the subject of these prayers "Prodigal." Underscores would look clunky. Pronouns would become wearisome. And "my addict" or "our addicts" lent strength to the wrong identity. So—prodigal—wasteful, wandering, lost. But the greatest characteristic of the prodigal in Luke 15, a detail woven into the prodigal's identity, is that the prodigal returned home.

By identifying the people we pray for as "Prodigal," we cling to this promise: the Prodigal returns to the arms of the Father.

Reading You Your
Messiah Rights

YOU HAVE THE RIGHT TO TELL GOD HOW YOU FEEL. Nothing you say will be used against you. You have the right for your case to be heard. You cannot afford your freedom, so your bond has been provided for you. Do you understand the rights I have just read to you? With these rights in mind, do you wish to pray?

Lord,

I pray Your favor upon Prodigal. Be his battle cry and rear guard. As he walks through the Valley of the Shadow of Death, light Prodigal's way and protect him from the assaults of the enemy. May angel armies surround him on all sides. May his weapon be Your words and Scriptural promises ringing in his ear. When Prodigal passes through danger unharmed, may hindsight reveal to Prodigal the undeniable proof of your presence. Amen.

Dear God,

_____
_____
_____
_____
_____
_____
_____
_____
_____
_____
_____
_____
_____
_____
_____
_____
_____
_____
_____
_____

Evidence of the Answer:

_____
_____
_____
_____
_____

For the Prodigal Who Is Praying

Heavenly Father,

As I embark on this journey, please stay steadfast at my side. Allow me to feel Your presence as painful and uncomfortable truths are revealed. As agonizing realizations are made, remind me of who You are, Father, and who I am in You. Hold my hand and walk through this journey with me, preparing each step for me. Rejoice with me in my victories and comfort me in my pain. Guide my heart and mind to be open to receive what You have to say. Strengthen me to withstand the pain that will come after. Heal what is broken Father.

Provide me and intentional and specific blessing through this process. I am not here by coincidence. You have divinely led me to this journey with you for a reason. May I learn what You have for me to learn and hear what You have for me to hear. By Your grace and mercy I beg for healing Protect me and comfort my soul in ways only You can. I pray all these things in Jesus' powerful name. *Amen.*

Lord,

May I be still, and aware of your presence here beside me. Assure me you do not hide your face from me, even now, in the midst of this trial. Let my words to you be honest and true, allowing you within my broken heart. Tear down every barrier remaining between us and remind me that You long to bring light into every dark situation. *Amen.*

Dear God,

_____

_____

_____

_____

_____

_____

_____

_____

_____

_____

_____

_____

_____

_____

_____

_____

_____

_____

_____

Evidence of the Answer:

_____

_____

_____

_____

Serenity Prayer

The fear of the LORD is the beginning of knowledge,
but fools despise wisdom and instruction.

Proverbs 1:7 NIV

God, grant me the serenity
To accept the things I cannot change,
The courage to change the things I can,
And the wisdom to know the difference.

Reinhold Niebuhr, 1934

Dear God,

_____
_____
_____
_____
_____
_____
_____
_____
_____
_____
_____
_____
_____
_____
_____
_____
_____
_____

Evidence of the Answer:

_____
_____
_____
_____
_____

A Prayer for the Person Praying

*Remember to welcome strangers, because some who have done
this have welcomed angels without knowing it.*

Hebrews 13:2 NCV

Come on, God.

Loving someone with an active addiction is so hard. Helplessness overwhelms me. I want to fix things, but not enable. The godly love in me wants to support Prodigal, and the sinner in me wants Prodigal to witness the entirety of the consequences of their choices for those around them. I love Prodigal but hate the person addiction turned Prodigal into.

As I pray for Prodigal, help me to press into grace rather than judge. Grant me peace as I mourn who Prodigal was before the addiction and help me accept that Prodigal is forever changed. Give me strength and courage to meet Prodigal in the midst of the struggle, and help me make room for the messy and imperfect. Grant me wisdom as I navigate life through prayer. Meet me in the dark. *Amen.*

Dear God,

_____

_____

_____

_____

_____

_____

_____

_____

_____

_____

_____

_____

_____

_____

_____

_____

_____

_____

_____

Evidence of the Answer:

_____

_____

_____

_____

_____

God's Behind-the-Scenes Love

When they came to Emmaus, he acted as if he was going on ahead. But they urged him, saying, "Stay with us. It's nearly evening, and the day is almost over." So he went in to stay with them. After he took his seat at the table with them, he took the bread, blessed and broke it, and gave it to them. Their eyes were opened and they recognized him, but he disappeared from their sight.

Luke 24:28-31 CEB

Dear God,

When we broke fellowship with You— before we even comprehended the weight of our sin, You died on the cross to protect us. Now I pray that same intuitive love into the life of Prodigal. Prodigal has pushed away everyone who loves him. He wants nothing to do with the church or his family and friends— the people who care. None of us are able to reach him. But You can. You are strong enough. Please step into the darkness, God. Step into the dirty corners—into the drug deals and the drama and the danger. Stand between Prodigal and people who intend to hurt him. Spill the last of the liquid to the floor. Be the soldier who guards his back, and pave the way for his search and rescue when he can't see a way out himself. Thank you for loving us even when we don't love You in return. *Amen.*

Dear God,

_____
_____
_____
_____
_____
_____
_____
_____
_____
_____
_____
_____
_____
_____
_____
_____
_____
_____
_____
_____

Evidence of the Answer:

_____
_____
_____
_____
_____

Ashley Worrell

HEY Y'ALL... I'M ASHLEY. As a young adult, I thought I had it all—a C-suite job in HR. Nice paycheck. Beautiful home. Perfect family. And a growing dependence on an evening glass of wine. And then three. And then... more. When I left that job I thought I loved, uprooted and moved home, and threw out the ever-present bottle in my fridge, I came to the end of myself. I don't know how to put the feeling into words when you throw away a crutch like alcohol and experience the full burden of guilt and shame. Whatever exists below rock bottom (liquid magma?) that's where I was. And that's where God met me. I begged God to show me my life still had purpose... and that night I dreamed the idea for a book which became *The Radiance of the Moon*.

I pursued the traditional-publishing route for a few paces, until God reminded me the obedience was in sharing the story—not chasing the book deal dream. By allowing God to guide my steps, I've remained on the path of sobriety and have been blessed ten-fold. When I get messages from readers all over the world who identify with my characters' deep struggles, it reminds me God is still with me and gave me a gift to depict feelings in stories that readers experience in real life but can't put into words themselves.

If I could say one thing to you it would be this: there is a path only you can walk, people only you can reach, words only you can speak. God loves the broken. I am one of them. Just a girl, with some words, and a page. But I am loved. Healed. And forgiven. I hope if you read my stories, that is what you will find.

I pray you find hope.

Love,
Ashley (the Second-Chance Storyteller)

Meeting Christ

As the deer pants for streams of water, so my soul pants for you, my God. My soul thirsts for God, for the living God. When can I go and meet with God My tears have been my food day and night, while people say to me all day long, "Where is your God?" These things I remember as I pour out my soul: how I used to go to the house of God under the protection of the Mighty One with shouts of joy and praise among the festive throng.

Why, my soul, are you downcast? Why so disturbed within me? Put your hope in God, for I will yet praise him, my Savior and my God.

Psalm 42:1-5, NIV

Veni Creator Spiritus, Come Creator Spirit,

Jesus are you there? My throat is parched with the need for whiskey. I don't even know who I am anymore. I keep trying to make things right on my own, but I keep making them worse. I've taken on traits of a person I swore I'd never be. A miserable sinner, wasting opportunities. I've been running from myself. I'm scared to let go because I feel so unworthy of redemption. I know I can't change the past. I know I need to trust you with my future. Please light my way.

To You, I come. I'm removing my boots to stand on holy ground. I'm laying down my sword to stop fighting against you. My battle-scarred, outstretched arms are begging for your mercy. Help me to be still and stop fighting. Help me to know that the battle is already won. That you have claimed the victory. I have nothing to offer you. But God, please save me. *Amen.*

Excerpt from Radiance of the Moon

Dear God,

_____

_____

_____

_____

_____

_____

_____

_____

_____

_____

_____

_____

_____

_____

_____

_____

_____

_____

_____

Evidence of the Answer:

_____

_____

_____

_____

_____

Gardener
and the *Phoenix*

I've foolishly believed time and again
That I author my life, that I hold the pen.
"Life to the fullest," God wanted for me,
So I contrived and I scribbled and I wrote fervently.
But the stories never ended the way I planned—
Tragedies invaded the script in my hand.

Outside in the garden, I threw my effort to the fire,
My hopes and my dreams and all I aspired.
With the weighted knowledge
Life would ne'er be the same
I watched dark smoke chortle up from the flames.

I awoke the next morning, drenched in grief
Empty of tears, but starved of relief.
I peeked out the window to witness dawn of new day
And saw a form near the ashes through vanishing haze.

The gardener crouched, with moisture in his eyes
And scattered the ashes as he silently cried.
Then I heard him speaking into the still
His voice, hands, heart manifested his will.
His tears landed like crystal seeds
And where each drop fell, a sprout conceived.
He patted the soil with gentle grace,
And from the ashes, beauty rose in its place.

He lowered himself against a tree.
Withdrawing parchment and ink,
He scrawled against his knees.
Not simply a gardener, I realized,
The Creator, Redeemer, the Author of Life.

I rushed to the garden. I knelt at his feet.
I surrendered the pen I'd been tempted to keep.
"Write me broken, devastated, scared and confused.
Write me lonely, battered, exhausted and bruised."

He laughed at my request, which I didn't expect,
And laid aside his story to straighten the facts.
"I'll write you bold, brave, strong, artistic and kind.
I'll write you tender, steadfast, generous and wise.
Battle-scarred, perhaps, but as always with us
Blessing awaits on this side of trust."

I stared over his shoulder at the illustration he'd drawn.
Glorious, exquisite, blazing brawn.
"Tragedy with my ink is blessing blurred in disguise.
I've depicted you as a phoenix.
From these ashes we'll rise."

Sanctuary for the Addict

Indeed, we felt we had received the sentence of death. But this happened that we might not rely on ourselves but on God, who raises the dead. He has delivered us from such a deadly peril, and he will deliver us again. On him we have set our hope that he will continue to deliver us, as you help us by your prayers. Then many will give thanks on our behalf for the gracious favor granted us in answer to the prayers of many.

2 Corinthians 1:9-11 NIV

Dear God,

Please provide sanctuary for Prodigal, whether it's a long drive, or mindless work, or a shower, please provide Prodigal with a place where she feels safe, where she can rest her heart, where she feels echoes of peace despite all the chaos around her. Give her sanctuary from the addiction. Grant her asylum from the danger she faces. And when she finds herself and is still in quiet place, I pray that she would be vulnerable enough to meet you there. May she see Your face and recognize Your love for her. *Amen.*

Dear God,

_____

_____

_____

_____

_____

_____

_____

_____

_____

_____

_____

_____

_____

_____

_____

_____

_____

_____

_____

_____

Evidence of the Answer:

_____

_____

_____

_____

_____

Forgive Me for Judging Addicts

If you forgive others their sins, your heavenly Father will also forgive you. But if you don't forgive others, neither will your Father forgive your sins.
Matthew 6:14-15 CEB

Heavenly Father,

Every addict is different, has a different process, a different journey. Sometimes I see another addict and I do not agree on their path to recovery. Jesus, please remind me that no two recovery journeys are the same. Please stop me, Father, when I have judgy thoughts. Remind me of the grace and mercy You freely give me every day. May my heart be compelled to pray for that addict instead of passing judgment, as I despise when people pass judgment on me. I know my recovery journey. Not theirs. I know how hard and devastating my recovery has been, but I know nothing about someone else's. Even addicts I love and have known for a lifetime protect secrets I don't know and live in a darkness of their own making. Thank you for my own recovery journey and all the prayers offered on my behalf. Thank you for the grace shown to me. *Amen.*

Dear God,

_____

_____

_____

_____

_____

_____

_____

_____

_____

_____

_____

_____

_____

_____

_____

_____

_____

Evidence of the Answer:

_____

_____

_____

_____

_____

Healthy Boundaries for Those Who Love the Prodigal

Praise be to the God and Father of our Lord Jesus Christ, the Father of compassion and the God of all comfort, who comforts us in all our troubles, so that we can comfort those in any trouble with the comfort we ourselves receive from God. For just as we share abundantly in the sufferings of Christ, so also our comfort abounds through Christ.

2 Corinthians 1:3-5 NIV

Dear God,

Every time I see Prodigal straying away from a healthy life, my heart breaks. I struggle when I see another addict struggling. I want to wrap my arms around them and tell them I understand. But I don't. Their choices create a vortex that swallow sanity, reason, wisdom, and, oftentimes, safety.

Jesus, help my heart. I feel like such a terrible person for having to set these boundaries! God, help me love this person from afar for now. Repeat to me that protecting my own safety does not mean I do not care. Show me appropriate and wise actions to take. I love Prodigal but his choices are dangerous for me and I cannot allow my safety to be jeopardized. Please strengthen my heart. *Amen.*

Dear God,

_____
_____
_____
_____
_____
_____
_____
_____
_____
_____
_____
_____
_____
_____
_____
_____
_____
_____
_____
_____

Evidence of the Answer:

_____
_____
_____
_____
_____

Prisoner of Addiction

This is what God the LORD says— the Creator of the heavens, who stretches them out, who spreads out the earth with all that springs from it, who gives breath to its people, and life to those who walk on it: "I, the LORD, have called you in righteousness; I will take hold of your hand. I will keep you and will make you to be a covenant for the people and a light for the Gentiles, to open eyes that are blind, to free captives from prison and to release from the dungeon those who sit in darkness.

Isaiah 42:5-7 NIV

Dear Chain-breaker,

Be with those in the darkness of addiction. I know firsthand how alone they feel. How shame creeps in. I understand the feeling of dwelling on all the ways you've hurt the people you love. And I know the idea of questioning yourself:

Am I good enough? If people knew the real me, they would never speak to me again. There's no way they would forgive me for the despicable things I've done.

The shame of using launches Prodigal back into the addiction to numb the pain. The cycle is maddening for Prodigal whose desire to quit is greater than anything, except his desire to use. The cycle is nearly impossible to escape. God, this is where you step in. You are the breaker of chains, defender of the weak. You are a strong fortress. You are the embodiment of victory. Please step into the fray and be Prodigal's champion. *Amen.*

Dear God,

_____
_____
_____
_____
_____
_____
_____
_____
_____
_____
_____
_____
_____
_____
_____
_____
_____
_____
_____

Evidence of the Answer:

_____
_____
_____
_____
_____

Hostage of Shame and Guilt

And now those young mock me in song; I have become a byword among them. They detest me and keep their distance; they do not hesitate to spit in my face. They advance as through a gaping breach; amid the ruins they come rolling in. Terrors overwhelm me; my dignity is driven away as by the wind, my safety vanishes like a cloud.

Job 30:9-10, 14-15 NIV

Hear me, oh Lord.

For I am oppressed and afflicted, struck at from every side. I am bound tightly by the memories of my past, the knowledge of sin, the dark crimson blemish of shame. I am surrounded by people who have no idea the depths of things that I've done, who do not seem to understand the potent power of a memory. Like trudging through quicksand, I feel myself dragged into the remembrance of my mistakes, the things I have done, the things I have left undone, and the people I have hurt.

I reach for you, and there in the wilderness you meet me. Your strong hands encircle mine, pulling me upward toward you. Behind me, Satan claws at my rib cage, trying to reclaim me, but you hold me fast. You calm my wildly beating heart and whisper assurance—when I was dead in my sin, you made me alive with you. None of this depends on me. It never did. You wipe the tears of grief from my eyes, and kiss my cheeks, reminding me you freed me.

Where once I medicated with substance, I now meditate on you, who you are, your presence—with your unexplainable peace. Help me oh Lord. Remove the oppressive weight of my shame. May I be ever reminded that you are not repelled by my sin as you carry me to redemption. *Amen.*

Dear God,

_____
_____
_____
_____
_____
_____
_____
_____
_____
_____
_____
_____
_____
_____
_____
_____
_____
_____
_____
_____

Evidence of the Answer:

_____
_____
_____
_____

Moments of Joy and Sobriety

The thief comes only to steal and kill and destroy; I have come that they may have life, and have it to the full.

John 10:10 NIV

Dear God,

I pray that Prodigal would have a sober day today. May she see the world around her through a clear lens and find joy in the simple things. May the sun burn brighter, the grass shine greener. Please give Prodigal's heart rest from all her striving and her suffering and the thoughts that overwhelm her. Give her a break from the torture of addiction today. Help her get things done, talk with friends, and feel accomplished, so when her head hits the pillow tonight she can say, "wow today was a really good day." I pray these moments of joy and sobriety in the midst of addiction might give Prodigal courage to succeed with sobriety again tomorrow. May she feel empowered by these days of happiness. *Amen.*

Dear God,

_____
_____
_____
_____
_____
_____
_____
_____
_____
_____
_____
_____
_____
_____
_____
_____
_____
_____
_____
_____

Evidence of the Answer:

_____
_____
_____
_____
_____

JESUS DOESN'T SAY SO in Luke 15,
but the Prodigal Son bawled his eyes out.
I know, because you can't step from your
darkest place into the safest rest of the
greatest love without breaking in between.

Clint Evans, *The Prodigal's Son:*
Crackhead to Jesus Freak

I am the good shepherd; I know my sheep and my sheep know me— just as the Father knows me and I know the Father—and I lay down my life for the sheep. I have other sheep that are not of this sheep pen. I must bring them also. They too will listen to my voice, and there shall be one flock and one shepherd.

John 10:14-16 NIV

Kindly Shepherd,

You call out for me, the lost one who has wandered from the flock. In my wandering I hear the gentle sound of your voice. It is ancient and holy, and you call me by name. I recognize you as you speak and I am filled with joy. I run to you, to the safety at your side. You bend toward me, Merciful One, and touch my heart. You know me and everything about me. You know each triumph, and each failure. You smile and shake your head because nothing I do takes you by surprise.

Father, we walk in the cool of the day. You sturdy me with your rod and staff helping me to breathe in the blessing of your presence. I do not have to impress you. I do not have to pretend that I wasn't lost only moments ago. I only need to walk by your side in this moment as you speak with me. There is no one like my shepherd. No one knows me so well. May I always find joy in your presence, comfort in your direction, my friend and companion. *Amen.*

Dear God,

_____
_____
_____
_____
_____
_____
_____
_____
_____
_____
_____
_____
_____
_____
_____
_____
_____
_____
_____

Evidence of the Answer:

_____
_____
_____
_____
_____

For a Homeless Heart to Find Belonging

For the message of the cross is foolishness to those who are perishing, but to us who are being saved it is the power of God.
1 Corinthians 1:18 NIV

Dear God,

I strived to belong to the wrong escapes, the wrong friends, the wrong purpose. I pray Lord for you to raise up a supportive community around me, of those whom I can be open and honest with, and who will accept and support me on my journey towards sobriety. May they have ears that listen, words of encouragement, and hearts that will accept me as you and I take strides into a new life. As I search for community and belonging, remind me that I always belong at your side. You have called me by name. I hear your voice. Clear away the noise so I can listen and continue to follow. *Amen.*

Dear God,

_____

_____

_____

_____

_____

_____

_____

_____

_____

_____

_____

_____

_____

_____

_____

_____

_____

_____

_____

_____

Evidence of the Answer:

_____

_____

_____

_____

_____

Drinking to Drown Out Demons and Regret

The joyful timbrels are stilled, the noise of revelers has stopped, the joyful harp is silent. No longer do they drink wine with song; the beer is bitter to its drinkers.

In the streets they cry out for wine; all joy turns to gloom, all joyful sounds are banished from the earth. The city is left in ruins, its gate is battered to pieces.

Isaiah 24:8-9, 11-12 NIV

Dear God,

You know why I drink. I'm trying to chase away the demons that haunt me when I'm sober. When I'm clean, the past boils over and I can't escape remembering all the terrible mistakes I've made. The only way to quiet the demons is to drink. People tell me there's a better way, but I don't believe them. They tell me You can help me, that with You I can be sober. But I don't know if I can live with my sobriety—sober me. The thought of pouring the whiskey down the drain terrifies me. God, if You're willing, You're gonna need to step in the middle of this. I need You. I need to more than just believe You will help me. I need You to prove You will help. I don't know what that looks like. I don't know what I'm asking. I just know I'm at the end of my rope. I don't wanna do this anymore, but sobriety terrifies me. What will I have in place of the drink, God? Are you real? Can you really help me? I'm willing to try anything, but I'm skeptical. I don't have enough faith without Your help. *Amen.*

Dear God,

_____
_____
_____
_____
_____
_____
_____
_____
_____
_____
_____
_____
_____
_____
_____
_____
_____
_____
_____
_____

Evidence of the Answer:

_____
_____
_____
_____

Demon of Unworthiness

Now this is what the LORD says.
He created you, people of Jacob;
he formed you, people of Israel.
He says, "Don't be afraid, because I have saved you.
I have called you by name, and you are mine.
When you pass through the waters, I will be with you.
When you cross rivers, you will not drown.
When you walk through fire, you will not be burned,
nor will the flames hurt you.
This is because I, the LORD, am your God,
the Holy One of Israel, your Savior.

Isaiah 43:1-3a CEV

Lord,

I know what your Word says about me—that I'm a child of yours. But right now, the enemy is shouting in my ear that I'm no good, I'm worthless, that you don't love me because of the mountain of sins. So, Lord, I come to you today asking you to renew my mind, to whisper in my ear that I am worthy, that I am good, that I have been saved by your grace. Please drown out the shouting with your loving whispers and remind me that no matter how much I've messed up in the past, and in the future, that you still love me. I really need you, Lord, to carry me and love me right now. *Amen.*

Dear God,

_____
_____
_____
_____
_____
_____
_____
_____
_____
_____
_____
_____
_____
_____
_____
_____
_____
_____
_____

Evidence of the Answer:

_____
_____
_____
_____
_____

PTSD, Trauma, and Childhood Hurts

All my closest friends despise me; the ones I have loved turn against me.

My bones cling to my skin and flesh; I have escaped by the skin of my teeth. Pity me. Pity me. You're my friends. God's hand has truly struck me. Why do you pursue me like God does, always hungry for my flesh?

Oh, that my words were written down, inscribed on a scroll with an iron instrut and lead, forever engraved on stone. But I know that my redeemer is alive and afterward he'll rise upon the dust. After my skin has been torn apart this way— then from my flesh I'll see God, whom I'll see myself— my eyes see, and not a stranger's. I am utterly dejected.

Job 19:19-27 CEB

Jesus,

Today my heart feels so heavy. The worst days of my life replay in slow motion like I am living them all over again. I can't close my eyes. Satan digs his nails into my shoulders. He hisses reminders of hurts others inflicted on me, and he accuses me of things that are not true, labels I used to wear. Victim. Worthless. Disappointment—and far worse. When I close my eyes, I relive the most painful moments I lived through.

Surround me Jesus. Chase Satan from me. Remind me of the new names You call me: Child, Beloved, Redeemed, Sanctified. Help me to release the pain in my past and to take hold of the hope you have called me to. Enable me to see the beauty you will bring from past pain, the tears of mine that didn't fall in vain. Fill me with your peace that passes all understanding, and help me to walk into newness of life. *Amen.*

Dear God,

_____
_____
_____
_____
_____
_____
_____
_____
_____
_____
_____
_____
_____
_____
_____
_____
_____
_____
_____

Evidence of the Answer:

_____
_____
_____
_____
_____

Spiritual Warfare

Finally, be strong in the Lord and in his mighty power.
Put on the full armor of God, so that you can take your
stand against the devil's schemes.

Ephesians 6:10-11 NIV

God,

Get high! Don't get high! Get high! Don't get high! Each exclamation slaps my right cheek and then the left. I want to use but I don't want to use. I feel You moving. You're working in me. You're slowly changing me away from the drug dependent addict I used to be. For the first time in my life, I feel hope that maybe things can be different. But every time I step out in faith to be sober, to trust you, Satan and his minions are right there, dogging every step, dragging me down. They cover my mouth so I can't praise You. They bind my feet so I can't run to You. I want to be free from the demons I carry with me everywhere I go. These sins that weigh me down. Satan doesn't want me to be healed. I don't feel threatening to Satan, but maybe he knows something I don't. Give me strength and courage to fight the enemy. Surround me with friends who will cover me in prayer. Uncover my mouth and embolden me to testify of how You have worked in my life. *Amen.*

Dear God,

_____
_____
_____
_____
_____
_____
_____
_____
_____
_____
_____
_____
_____
_____
_____
_____
_____
_____
_____
_____

Evidence of the Answer:

_____
_____
_____
_____
_____

No Greater Love

I want this poem to reach
Deep to the heart of you.
I wish my words could edit your life,
And heal all your hidden wounds.
If I could rewrite your pain,
And all that goes unsaid,
I would backspace the brokenness,
And Ctrl-V "unscathed" instead.

I wish my words could write you out
Of the trouble that you know.
"The dragon lay slain
By the valiant hero."
While my words cannot pull you out,
Because they have no power
I can recount the narrative of Christ—
Hero and editor.

He fought to free you from the chains
That contract around your soul.
His life, His breath, His love for you,
Are stronger than you know.
He depicted you as wonderful,
The delight of your Father's eyes.
You're so precious to the Lord Most High
That He left His throne behind.

My words have no authority,
But His Word calmed the raging sea.

With His prose the world was formed,
Nature bends its knee.
Stars shine to please Him
He doesn't seek them for reviews.
And though His grandeur is unfathomable,
He is never far from you.

This Author who composed the tide,
And deleted death from life
Can, with His Words, ease your pain,
And calm the raging storm inside.
Surrender to Him, just let go,
Free fall into His page
And when you land on gentle hands,
You'll recognize His grace.

Since my words are feeble, frail,
Grossly insufficient
I will sing to you the Savior's song
And pray that you will listen.
"Come to me you weary,
And I will give you rest.
My peace I leave, my peace I give,
Freely breathe my Spirit breath.

"You're free, you are forgiven child,
Satan can't hold you in the past
Don't let those demons define you, child.
You are worthy to be blessed.
I bind up the broken-hearted,
By my stripes I heal you.
No greater love has a man than this,
Than the love I have for you."

Fatigue

Don't you know? Haven't you heard?
The LORD is the everlasting God,
the creator of the ends of the earth.
He doesn't grow tired or weary.
His understanding is beyond human reach,
giving power to the tired
and reviving the exhausted.
Youths will become tired and weary,
young will certainly stumble;
but those who hope in the LORD
will renew their strength;
they will fly up on wings like eagles;
they will run and not be tired;
they will walk and not be weary.

Isaiah 40:28-31 CEB

Lord Jesus,

Staying clean in the midst of struggles and painful situations is harder than most realize. Father I need you every hour I need you. Every moment I need you. Fear sweeps through my heart as my addiction bubbles to the surface, and the urge to numb it all grows. Hold my hand, Jesus, and guide me through this mine field of life. Remind me it is okay not to be okay and remind me who I am in you, Father. Remind me of my strength when I feel too weak to go on. Remind me of my purpose in your Kingdom and that I am more loved than I know. Protect me from my thoughts and fears, Lord, and allow me a sound mind and a full heart. *Amen.*

Dear God,

_____

_____

_____

_____

_____

_____

_____

_____

_____

_____

_____

_____

_____

_____

_____

_____

Evidence of the Answer:

_____

_____

_____

_____

Collateral Damage

God so loved the world that he gave his only Son, so that everyone who believes in him won't perish but will have eternal life. God didn't send his Son into the world to judge the world, but that the world might be saved through him.

John 3:16-17 CEB

Dear Jesus,

With tear-stained eyes I am on my knees, Father. My heart is broken, shattered into a million pieces. This disease of addiction has stripped the prodigal I love of so much. My heart breaks for the strain Prodigal's drug use places on our family. How do you do it God? How do you love us so much and never leave us, yet watch us and allow us to make destructive decision after destructive decision? Your heart must break! And yet, your love never fades, never leaves.

Teach me to love like that! Teach my heart to have the strength to love when it's hard to love, when the other person does not want to receive my love. To maintain healthy boundaries and not enable bad behavior but also be supportive. Jesus, heal my heart and the heart of Prodigal. *Amen.*

Dear God,

_____
_____
_____
_____
_____
_____
_____
_____
_____
_____
_____
_____
_____
_____
_____
_____
_____
_____
_____

Evidence of the Answer:

_____
_____
_____
_____
_____

Knowing When to Ask for Help

Simon, Simon, Satan has asked to sift all of you as wheat.
But I have prayed for you, Simon, that your faith may not fail.
And when you have turned back, strengthen your brothers.

Luke 22:31-32 NIV

Alright, God.

You win. I tried it my way. Tried doing it on my own. Failed, 100%. Now I'm flat on my back and need help. I don't want to ask for help because I'm scared people will say, "I told you so," and I don't wanna hear it. I'm afraid of judgment. If I ask for help, I'm admitting I have a problem. I hate feeling weak! But I can't ignore the fact that I feel weak. This drug is stronger than my own willpower. If I am going to succeed, then I need to step out of my own way. Help me set aside my pride and trust You to bring people into my life who will truly make a difference, who will love me for me no matter what mistakes I have made. *Amen.*

Dear God,

_____
_____
_____
_____
_____
_____
_____
_____
_____
_____
_____
_____
_____
_____
_____
_____
_____
_____
_____

Evidence of the Answer:

_____
_____
_____
_____

My son, if you accept my words
and store up my commands within you,
turning your ear to wisdom
and applying your heart to understanding—
indeed, if you call out for insight
and cry aloud for understanding,
and if you look for it as for silver
and search for it as for hidden treasure,
then you will understand the fear of the LORD
and find the knowledge of God.

Proverbs 2:1-5 NIV

Dear God,

Prodigal cannot do this on her own. She needs Your help and she needs help from people who love her. Please help Prodigal set her pride down so she can receive the help she needs. I can't imagine having to admit my faults so vulnerably, the way she'll be forced to do. So I pray for people to be receptive and tender hearted as they listen to her story. Please give Prodigal a safe place, a safe person to practice sharing her story with. Please help the people around her to be trustworthy with her heart. *Amen.*

Dear God,

_____
_____
_____
_____
_____
_____
_____
_____
_____
_____
_____
_____
_____
_____
_____
_____
_____
_____
_____
_____

Evidence of the Answer:

_____
_____
_____
_____
_____

Angry Addict

When they hurled their insults at him, he did not retaliate;
when he suffered, he made no threats. Instead, he entrusted
himself to him who judges justly.

1 Peter 2:23 NIV

Dear God,

Addiction stole Prodigal's sanity, her rational thought. Her anger flares at the touch of a trigger. She spews belligerent, venomous thoughts to me and the people who love her most. Her heart is gnarled with hatred. When Prodigal snarls, she reminds me of a wolf in a trap gnawing at its own leg. She is unapproachable and hostile, even to those who would help her. Did you experience people like this during Your time on earth, Jesus? People insulted You on Your way to Golgatha, (Matthew 27:39), as You hung on the cross.

What can I learn from Your response to them? What did you do? You did not allow Your purpose to be sidetracked by taking their bait. You pressed forward, and with each step You took toward the Father's will for You, You left them further behind. Drown out Prodigal's cruelty with the truth of Your love for me. Help me step forward in Your will for me as I die to myself. *Amen.*

Dear God,

_____

_____

_____

_____

_____

_____

_____

_____

_____

_____

_____

_____

_____

_____

_____

_____

_____

_____

Evidence of the Answer:

_____

_____

_____

_____

_____

Protection from Self-harm

God is our refuge and strength,
an ever-present help in trouble.
Therefore we will not fear, though the earth give way
and the mountains fall into the heart of the sea,
though its waters roar and foam
and the mountains quake with their surging.

There is a river whose streams make glad the city of God,
the holy place where the Most High dwells.
God is within her, she will not fall;
God will help her at break of day.

Psalm 46:1-5 NIV

Dear God,

I know I have scarred and damaged the body you have given me. Life becomes too much for me to bear, and I can't stop myself from putting the blade to my skin. I can't stop swallowing one more pill, snorting one more line, swallowing one more sip. I get so deep in my head I drown out your love and care. Dear God, I beg you to protect me from myself and to protect those around me from my actions. Show me how to move on from this cycle of harm and to find something new in its place. *Amen.*

Dear God,

_____
_____
_____
_____
_____
_____
_____
_____
_____
_____
_____
_____
_____
_____
_____
_____
_____
_____
_____

Evidence of the Answer:

_____
_____
_____
_____
_____

THE JUDGE SAID, "Does the prosecution have any objection to Mr. Evans' handcuffs being removed?"

"No, Your Honor."

An officer stepped forward. The only sound in the room was the click and jingle of metal.

Clint rubbed his wrists. "Thank you, Your Honor."

"The defendant should not speak to the judge unless spoken to," said the judge. "And, you're welcome."

The court reporter's mouth tipped up into a smile as she recorded the conversation.

The Prodigal's Son: Crackhead to Jesus Freak

Honesty & Vulnerability: Fighting Embarrassment

But I am a worm and not a person,
A disgrace of mankind and despised by the people.
All who see me deride me;
They sneer, they shake their heads, saying,
"Turn him over to the LORD; let Him save him;
Let Him rescue him, because He delights in him."

Psalm 22:6-8 NASB

Dear God,

I am so embarrassed about the choices I've made, choices I keep making. I'm such a screw up. I know I need to be honest with the people who care about me, but my addiction feels like an old friend, a close friend, and I don't know if I'm ready to say goodbye. And what's the point, anyway, if I'm just going to relapse—again? That will just pile on the embarrassment. "I want to get clean. Nope. Wait. Just kidding." If I want to be sober, I'll need a babysitter 24-7, and who has patience for that? I'll have to lay out all my secrets, tips and tricks I use to hide the contraband and sneak away. Am I ready? Am I willing to let go? I've used my vice for so long to cope with stress, what will I do when I run into a problem? Am I ready for this God? I'm almost ready. Please give me the courage and the opportunity to confess my desire for sobriety. *Amen.*

Dear God,

_____
_____
_____
_____
_____
_____
_____
_____
_____
_____
_____
_____
_____
_____
_____
_____
_____
_____

Evidence of the Answer:

_____
_____
_____
_____

Who is always in trouble?
Who argues and fights?
Who has cuts and bruises?
Whose eyes are red?
Everyone who stays up late,
having just one more drink.
Don't even look
at that colorful stuff
bubbling up in the glass!
It goes down so easily,
but later it bites
like a poisonous snake.

Proverbs 23:29-32 CEV

Dear God,

As special occasions come up please give my prodigal strength. Give her strength to stand solid in her sobriety but also be kind and gracious to those taking part in things she cannot. Allow her a non-judgmental heart and open her eyes to focus on what the occasion is celebrating instead of what she cannot do in those moments. Grant her spirit of peace and love. Allow those around her to be supportive and compassionate in those moments, and to recognize the inner turmoil she battles. *Amen.*

Dear God,

_____
_____
_____
_____
_____
_____
_____
_____
_____
_____
_____
_____
_____
_____
_____
_____
_____
_____
_____
_____
_____

Evidence of the Answer:

_____
_____
_____
_____

Discernment

For the LORD gives wisdom;
from his mouth come knowledge and understanding.
He holds success in store for the upright,
he is a shield to those whose walk is blameless,
for he guards the course of the just
and protects the way of his faithful ones.

Proverbs 2:6-8 NIV

Dear God,

I know you want me to be sober, but I don't know how you want me to stay sober. Sobriety feels impossible. There are triggers everywhere. My circumstances haven't changed. I live in the same house, hang out with the same friends, go to the same job. Staying sober with my life as it is won't work. There are too many chains holding me back. I feel like I need witness protection to hide from my addictions. Dear God, show me who I need to say goodbye to. Remove me from places and situations that are bad for me. Break my unbreakable chains and help me step out in faith to new life and godly inheritance, rooted in you. *Amen.*

Dear God,

_____
_____
_____
_____
_____
_____
_____
_____
_____
_____
_____
_____
_____
_____
_____
_____
_____
_____
_____
_____

Evidence of the Answer:

_____
_____
_____
_____
_____

Even if you think you can stand up to temptation, be careful not to fall. You are tempted in the same way that everyone else is tempted. But God can be trusted not to let you be tempted too much, and he will show you how to escape from your temptations. My friends, you must keep away from idols. I am speaking to you as people who have enough sense to know what I am talking about.

1 Corinthians 10:12-15 CEV

Lord,

This walk is one step at a time. Some days it feels like I will take things too fast, stumble and fall. Today was one of those days. I wished I could engage with the people and temptations with the strength of someone who has never experienced one day of addiction. And yet, you and I know better don't we? I call to mind your wisdom, "If your right eye causes you to sin, tear it out and throw it away. For it is better that you lose one of your members than that your whole body be thrown into hell." This is a strong instruction, a hard teaching. Yet I know that there are some things my flesh will never overcome. Give me courage, Lord, to tear out the things in my life that caused me to sin. Help me to walk away without looking back. I don't want to revisit the depths of hell that addiction plunged me into. Place boundary posts in my life around things that will keep me safe. Let me not wander away from your rod and staff, but keep me close to you. When others lure me toward sin, speak for me Lord, and hold me fast to your side. *Amen.*

Dear God,

_____
_____
_____
_____
_____
_____
_____
_____
_____
_____
_____
_____
_____
_____
_____
_____
_____
_____
_____

Evidence of the Answer:

_____
_____
_____
_____
_____

*Therefore, as God's chosen people, holy and dearly loved,
clothe yourselves with compassion, kindness, humility,
gentleness and patience.*

Colossians 3:12 NIV

Jesus, Strong Lion, Immortal and Invisible King,

I pray for Prodigal that she will know that not for a single moment was she ever unwanted. The world has devoured her, but I pray you break every lie that has been spoken over her. Restore to her the words you speak over her words like loved, healed, and forgiven. Take the burden from her shoulders, Lord. Carry her. I ask these things in the name of the father, son, and Holy Ghost. *Amen.*

Excerpt From Radiance of the Moon

Dear God,

_____

_____

_____

_____

_____

_____

_____

_____

_____

_____

_____

_____

_____

_____

_____

_____

_____

_____

_____

Evidence of the Answer:

_____

_____

_____

_____

My Grievances Against Prodigal

You call me 'Teacher' and 'Lord,' and you speak correctly,
because I am. If I, your Lord and teacher, have washed
your feet, you too must wash each other's feet. I have given
you an example: Just as I have done, you also must do.

John 13:13-15 CEV

Dear God,

That argument was pretty bad. I'm so tired of Prodigal's needs and selfishness trumping mine. Prodigal steals my peace, my joy, my time, my energy, and my money. Prodigal exhausts me and I don't know if I have what it takes to help Prodigal anymore. I'm so tired. Dear God, protect me. Speak to me. Show me what is right and how much to be involved. Help me define the space between boundaries and grace. Give me strength and courage to press forward in relationship with Prodigal, and show me what that looks like. Maybe it's a bed for the night one last time, and maybe it's prayer from a distance. I know You yearn for Prodigal to return home. Show me my place on Prodigal's journey. Speak clearly, so I don't mistake my own thoughts for Yours. Above all, please step into the damage we've done to one another and create space for reconciliation in the future. *Amen.*

Dear God,

_____
_____
_____
_____
_____
_____
_____
_____
_____
_____
_____
_____
_____
_____
_____
_____
_____
_____
_____

Evidence of the Answer:

_____
_____
_____
_____
_____

Traveler

She trudged along a wind-tossed road,
Loose gravel beneath bare feet.
Beside buffeted waves, in sea-salt air,
Through heat and hail and sleet.

A traveler journeyed near her.
He appeared as tired as she felt.
"Is this all we should expect of life?"
She murmured to herself.

The traveler frowned and shook his head.
"Sorry," she rolled her eyes.
"This life is leagues from my imagined dreams.
Reality has grayer skies.

"My feet are calloused, my dress is torn.
I don't recognize myself."
She uncurled her hands and showed the man
Blisters, cuts and welts.

He wrapped her wounds with linen of blue.
"When you've no safe place to land,
Let this Hope be the rope that anchors you:
I also have scarred hands.

You're stronger than you realize.
You've endurance to see this through.
Seems like you've forgotten
That I've never forgotten you."

Identity

For you created my inmost being;
you knit me together in my mother's womb.
I praise you because I am fearfully and wonderfully made;
your works are wonderful,
I know that full well.
My frame was not hidden from you
when I was made in the secret place,
when I was woven together in the depths of the earth.
Your eyes saw my unformed body;
all the days ordained for me were written in your book
before one of them came to be.

Psalm 139:13-16 NIV

Father,

You formed me within my mother's womb. No part of me was an accident. You knew before you formed light there would be me, right here, in the grand tapestry of your design. You knew what colors you would weave me with and where I would tear or fray. And yet you looked at your creation and you called it good. For years I tried to be something I am not, to wear the titles of things I am not, to participate in things less than what you want for me. Lord, I pray that I may see your original design. Help me to know the special threads you wove into my heart. Make known to me the gifts you placed in me with intention. Allow me to behold the beauty of your creation in me, and help me to believe you have called it good. *Amen.*

Dear God,

_____

_____

_____

_____

_____

_____

_____

_____

_____

_____

_____

_____

_____

_____

_____

_____

_____

_____

_____

_____

_____

_____

Evidence of the Answer:

_____

_____

_____

_____

_____

When an Addict Listens to Legitimate Grievances

If anyone has caused grief, he has not so much grieved me as he has grieved all of you to some extent—not to put it too severely. The punishment inflicted on him by the majority is sufficient. Now instead, you ought to forgive and comfort him, so that he will not be overwhelmed by excessive sorrow. I urge you, therefore, to reaffirm your love for him.

2 Corinthians 2:5-8 NIV

Lord,

At times it feels my past will never stay behind me. Someone I love shared with me how my actions, by way of my addiction, caused them to suffer. My carelessness, my choices. My heart is grieved, Lord, because in the middle of my addiction, I never considered anyone but myself. Help me accept their hard words. I fell short. I did harm. My actions created a chasm between me and the person I love. Give me courage to accept their grievances and to repent of the ways I caused them harm. If bridging the hurt is possible, show me the way.

Soften their heart toward me, as I try to walk in step with you. For the trespasses people cannot forgive, help me find acceptance. Although they keep record of my wrongs, your mercy is new every morning. Place in me a heart of humility, that I may follow your spirit into a new life of repentance. *Amen.*

Dear God,

_____

_____

_____

_____

_____

_____

_____

_____

_____

_____

_____

_____

_____

_____

_____

_____

_____

_____

_____

_____

Evidence of the Answer:

_____

_____

_____

_____

_____

Break Prodigal's Heart

I will give you a new heart and put a new spirit in you; I will remove from you your heart of stone and give you a heart of flesh. And I will put my Spirit in you and move you to follow my decrees and be careful to keep my laws.

Ezekiel 36:26-27 NIV

Sovereign Lord,

May prodigal hear Your Word penetrating through cracks in his heart. His life is in ruins. He's starving for goodness and truth, but doesn't know it. He's a disgrace, and rather than change or repent, he only hardens his armor. Break his heart for you God. Shatter Prodigal's man-made kingdom and the walls he hides behind. True change will only come from the power of your voice. Give Prodigal a new heart that beats for you, and move him to love and obey you. Amen.

Dear God,

_____

_____

_____

_____

_____

_____

_____

_____

_____

_____

_____

_____

_____

_____

_____

_____

_____

Evidence of the Answer:

_____

_____

_____

_____

Protect Prodigal from Judgmental Comments

Save me from the mud! Don't let me drown! Let me be saved from those who hate me and from these watery depths! Don't let me be swept away by the floodwaters! Don't let the abyss swallow me up! Don't let the pit close its mouth over me! Answer me, LORD, for your faithful love is good! Turn to me in your great compassion! Don't hide your face from me, your servant, because I'm in deep trouble. Answer me quickly! Come close to me! Redeem me! Save me because of my enemies!

Psalm 69:14-18 CEB

Dear God,

Please protect Prodigal from the impact of judgmental and negative comments from others. Please forgive me for the times I've hurt Prodigal with my words. When Prodigal owns these comments, he allows them to label him and define him. All his life you have been faithful. You love him. You love his heart. And you don't want him to be broken anymore. Tie the tongues of nay-sayers. Surround him only with people who speak hope and life into his heart. Help Prodigal to rise above what the haters say about him and cling to the truth. Your opinion is the only opinion that matters. And to you, Prodigal is beautiful. He is worthy. He is a work in progress, and his story is not finished yet. *Amen.*

Dear God,

_____
_____
_____
_____
_____
_____
_____
_____
_____
_____
_____
_____
_____
_____
_____
_____
_____
_____
_____
_____
_____
_____

Evidence of the Answer:

_____
_____
_____
_____
_____

The Addict's Reputation

See, I have refined you, but not like silver;
I have tested you in the furnace of misery.
For the sake of my reputation, for my own sake, I will act,
for why will my name be made impure?
I won't give my glory to another.

Isaiah 48:10-11 CEB

Dear God,

Decisions over time carve a person's reputation, the way water dictates the shape of a river. Reputation, good or bad, is the sum of decisions executed over time. I pray for Prodigal, destroying her reputation, one hit at a time. Lay the foundation for a good reputation and opportunities to make good choices. Give Prodigal the strength to step out in faith. Help others see her brokenness through Your eyes. May her reputation become a testimony of what you are doing in her life. Help her cling to the reputation and identity You have in store for her. *Amen.*

Dear God,

_____
_____
_____
_____
_____
_____
_____
_____
_____
_____
_____
_____
_____
_____
_____
_____
_____
_____
_____

Evidence of the Answer:

_____
_____
_____
_____

My Reputation Precedes Me

If you love those who love you, what reward will you get?
Are not even the tax collectors doing that? And if you
greet only your own people, what are you doing more than
others? Do not even pagans do that? Be perfect, therefore,
as your heavenly Father is perfect.

Matthew 5:46-48 NIV

Jesus,

Once again, my reputation has preceded me. In the logical part of my brain, I knew things I did in the dark would one day come to light, but oh how it hurts. Especially because reputation only matters to those who do not know me well. How I long to wipe my slate clean, to have upright standing in my community. Remind me of what I can control and what I can't. I cannot control how people perceive my past, or how they respond. Help me trust you are here with me, re-building my life. You alone ascribe my true worth. Help me react with forgiveness and kindness, even when others are unforgiving and un-kind to me. Where possible, help others know me and my heart before passing judgment upon me. Thank you for being a friend to me, a Sinner. *Amen.*

Dear God,

_____
_____
_____
_____
_____
_____
_____
_____
_____
_____
_____
_____
_____
_____
_____
_____
_____
_____

Evidence of the Answer:

_____
_____
_____
_____
_____

SMALL ACTS OF KINDNESS mattered.
They were God whispering, "You are loved."
Through these moments, God granted me
glimpses of life with Him, like He'd cracked
a window open of the life He prepared for
me and allowed me to peer inside.

Clint Evans, *The Prodigal's Son: Crackhead to Jesus Freak*

When an Addict Faces Grief

Lord, have mercy, because I am in misery.
My eyes are weak from so much crying,
and my whole being is tired from grief.
My life is ending in sadness,
and my years are spent in crying.
My troubles are using up my strength,
and my bones are getting weaker.

Psalm 31:9-10 NCV

Dear Jesus,

No one, no one, gets to tell me how to do this. Everyone is panicking over our loved one's death. Meanwhile, I am absolutely shattered. I know Grief. We didn't speak to one another for a long time, but when he returned, I recognized him. Grief is an opponent who plays with no holes barred.

I'm losing myself. The enormity of what lies before me—living life without my person— is an oppressive weight on my chest. I want to escape me, but I can't. The drug calls. Escape. Freedom. Forget. The desire to use is hammering against my skull and I want to cave. If I do, I will lose everything.

Jesus. Do you hear me? I can't do this on my own. These struggles are dragging me into the dirt. I'm five feet under and losing the fight. Maybe that's how it's supposed to be. Maybe soon I will join my friend. Jesus, rescue me! *Amen.*

Dear God,

_____

_____

_____

_____

_____

_____

_____

_____

_____

_____

_____

_____

_____

_____

_____

_____

_____

_____

Evidence of the Answer:

_____

_____

_____

_____

Buckling Beneath Responsibilities and Stress

Have I not commanded you? Be strong and courageous!
Do not be terrified nor dismayed, for the LORD your God
is with you wherever you go."
Joshua 1:9 NIV

Dear God,

I know I'm supposed to be strong, but my burdens are too heavy for me to bear the weight of right now. I feel like I'm falling behind and drowning in the weight of my responsibilities. Dear God, take these obstacles off my shoulders and make it so I can breathe again. Make it so that I can walk in your steps and do as you command of me without being weighed down by my mortal responsibilities that crush me. *Amen.*

Dear God,

_____
_____
_____
_____
_____
_____
_____
_____
_____
_____
_____
_____
_____
_____
_____
_____
_____
_____

Evidence of the Answer:

_____
_____
_____
_____
_____

Erin Niebuhr Hernandez

MY NAME IS ERIN. If you are reading these prayers, then addiction has touched you or someone you love in a significant way. This book is evidence of my victory and addiction, but even greater, these prayers are a love story of how my heavenly Father walked his daughter to a victory she never expected. My story is not unlike so many others and I hope through my sharing, prodigals will experience the love of God and find light rather than the darkness they've found themselves in.

Every addict has a specific vice that claws at them, shreds them to pieces from the inside out. Other drugs are a shoulder shrug. For instance, few people can snort a line of cocaine and walk away, but I did. I used drugs recreationally as a teenager. No big deal. Then, at a party, someone I trusted laced the cocaine with heroine and didn't tell me. That jumpstarted my journey of addiction.

> Sam was the first Christian who ever laid aside all judgments and asked what it felt like to be addicted, and how hard it was to get sober.

When I woke up the next morning, every cell in my body cried out with need. I spent the next 8 months using every means at my disposal to get my hands on more. I lived for the high and endured—survived—life in between. One morning, I woke up with my then fiancé, in a hotel room, surrounded by all sorts of drugs. I was jolted awake by the presence of the Holy Spirit. God said in a voice so crystal clear: "This is not who I created you to be. This is not the person you are, the mother you are. This is not the woman I created you to be. Get up and walk out". This is not what I wanted my life to look. My dad was a pastor. I knew about Jesus, but I'd shut Him out for longer than I would care to remember.

Heroine alters a person's body and they become not just addicted, but physically dependent on the drug. Quitting "heron" cold turkey is life-threatening. I learned that after my detox. Days two and three were the worst. Sweats, muscle cramping, stomach-convulsing, a brain-on-fire desire to end the misery by getting high. I writhed on the floor, I screamed, I swore. I tore my hair.

I truly believe I only survived the withdrawal by the grace of God. After the storm passed, I found that Jesus had been waiting there for me all along. The journey to recovery was neither short, nor straight. I'm a strong believer, and relapse is always one choice away. Now, I honor my Niebuhr family legacy of encouraging other addicts on their sobriety journey.

> I once asked my close friend, Pastor Clint Evans, "How'd you quit cigarettes cold turkey?"
>
> "Simple," he said. "I started smoking crack."

If you are a Prodigal steeped in addiction, know that I've been on my knees praying for your freedom. And if you are on the outside, watching a Prodigal you love tear his life to shreds, you have a place in this story, too.

When an Addict
is Hard to Live With

You have put me in the lowest pit,
in the darkest depths.
Your wrath lies heavily on me;
you have overwhelmed me with all your waves.
You have taken from me my closest friends
and have made me repulsive to them.
I am confined and cannot escape;
my eyes are dim with grief.

I call to you, LORD, every day;
I spread out my hands to you.

Psalm 88:6-9 NIV

Oh, sweet Jesus,

Give me patience. I love Prodigal, and I am so proud of her sobriety. However, Prodigal is not an easy person to be around. Right now, she is judgmental, hurtful, and selfish—and emotional. She is so focused on her journey that she is unable to show compassion or grace to those who do not see things the way she does. She does not have the capacity to accept the difference in others' sobriety journeys or life choices. Soften her heart, Lord, and open Prodigal's eyes to see others the way You do. Allow her to step outside of herself. Bring prodigal back to those who love her, Father. Hold her hand when she is unsteady and although she has come out of the darkness, allow her to walk in your light. *Amen.*

Dear God,

_____

_____

_____

_____

_____

_____

_____

_____

_____

_____

_____

_____

_____

_____

_____

_____

_____

_____

_____

Evidence of the Answer:

_____

_____

_____

_____

Facing Fears

But Jesus continued looking around to see who had touched him. The woman, knowing that she was healed, came and fell at Jesus' feet. Shaking with fear, she told him the whole truth. Jesus said to her, "Dear woman, you are made well because you believed. Go in peace; be healed of your disease."
Mark 5:32-34 CEV

Lord,

I am in fear right now. I'm afraid of ... everything. I'm afraid of not having enough money, not being healthy, not being a good spouse, not being a good father, a good grandfather. I lay awake at night churning those fears and others. I have the head knowledge of what your Word says about fear and worry and anxiety. I do.

So, Lord, in this moment, I need a touch of peace about just one thing that I'm afraid of. Just one. So I can truly believe with all my heart that all will be okay. I need that, Lord. Just one thing. Doesn't matter which one. Any will do. I know you've shown in mercy, your grace, your power, your love before. But I need it again, Lord. Badly. Please quiet my mind, so I can see and hear your work in me. Thank you, Lord. *Amen.*

Dear God,

_____
_____
_____
_____
_____
_____
_____
_____
_____
_____
_____
_____
_____
_____
_____
_____
_____
_____
_____
_____

Evidence of the Answer:

_____
_____
_____
_____
_____

The Pain an Addict Feels

*Then I looked again at all the acts of oppression which
were being done under the sun. And behold, I saw the
tears of the oppressed and that they had no one to comfort
them; and power was on the side of their oppressors,
but they had no one to comfort them.*

Ecclesiastes 4:1 NASB

Jesus, Man of Sorrows,

To the one so acquainted with grief and pain,

Be near to me now. Lord I ache. I long to numb my brokenness. You watched as I am tossed and shaken, you collected each of my tears in a bottle. There is so little I know for sure except for this—you are for me. Just as the rain and snow come down and do not return to void of purpose, I know you are bringing something beautiful out of this pain. You surround me with your presence, you hold me still. You assure me that feeling pain is productive, it will bring forth re-birth in me. In that day, just as a mother who labored for her child, I will feel the joy of your endurance and love.

Sometimes there's nothing anyone can say. The wind blows where it wishes, we know the sound and yet we are helpless to explain where it comes from or where it is going. So it is with my heart. I cannot explain this pain I feel. Lord listen to my heart cry in each tear. Hold steadfast and from this pain, bring great joy. *Amen.*

Dear God,

_____
_____
_____
_____
_____
_____
_____
_____
_____
_____
_____
_____
_____
_____
_____
_____
_____
_____

Evidence of the Answer:

_____
_____
_____
_____
_____

Self-esteem

For the word of God is living and active, and sharper than any two-edged sword, even penetrating as far as the division of soul and spirit, of both joints and marrow, and able to judge the thoughts and intentions of the heart. And there is no creature hidden from His sight, but all things are open and laid bare to the eyes of Him to whom we must answer. Therefore, since we have a great high priest who has passed through the heavens, Jesus the Son of God, let's hold firmly to our confession.

Hebrews 4:12-14 NASB

Dear God,

Continue to work on the heart of Prodigal. Obliterate the shame seeded in him as a child.

You are a piece of garbage.

You are worthless.

No one wants you.

You are unloveable.

These are the lies he begs to be silenced. Clear his heart of these wrong perceptions and grant him the grace to see himself the way that others do. In your mercy, reveal to him what you see when you look at him. Jesus, you are the only one with the power to slay these misconceptions in his heart. Jesus, Prodigal is a man worth fighting for.

Use Your sword. Be sharp and quick. Let Prodigal's remaining heartbeats on this earth know, intimately, Your joy and freedom.

Let it be so. *Amen.*

Dear God,

_____

_____

_____

_____

_____

_____

_____

_____

_____

_____

_____

_____

_____

_____

_____

_____

_____

Evidence of the Answer:

_____

_____

_____

_____

_____

Addict
at the Mic

Darkness shines on your own design
Trapped and afraid and left behind.
Lies repeat until they're true.
You're no good. You're alone. No one's coming for you.

The boy became a man but the lies are still inside
He constructed his life atop the shame he hides.
You're no good. You're alone. No one's coming for you.
Some people are worthy of love, but who are you?

Yet one small spark that darkness missed,
Transforms to flame—
A man with a mic to his lips.

Because the little boy was never alone.
There was a Great Big God present all along
Who graced the boy with the gift of song.

"You're muted now, child, but just you wait.
The world will hear your voice
And make no mistake.

I gifted you bass like thunder
To break the chains confining others.

Your smooth baritone sound
Will soothe weary souls

My love will verberate through
Your tenor and soprano

Darkness knows the power bursting inside of you
The second you step on stage, he knows he'll be through
He ambushes you and beats you down
But I know you by name and your gorgeous sound.

I believe in you.
You're more than good.
Your heart's been through more than one heart should.

I didn't have to find you. I've always been here.
I stood with you at your life's premiere.

I see you. I know you. You have worth.
Unmute the mic I handed you at birth.

I task you to chase away the lies that the others believe.
Belt my truth so they can't help but receive.

When you open your mouth, this is what you should say
(And don't be afraid. I rule this day.):

"You might be scared, but you're never alone.
You're good enough, you're worthy. God calls you His own."

Take it from the boy who hid in the dark
Whose God protected hope, that magical spark.
I believe in a God who believes in me.
Who erases every shame, who redeems, who frees.

We are more than our worst. We are called to live
A beautiful life that begins with this:

It starts with the lie you no longer believe
And crescendos with truth as the melody
Life change will come shortly thereafter
A descant of praise, a forte of laughter
Because our God raised from the grave
And our worship raises rafters.

No matter your song or your talent,
Unmute your mic
And stand steadfast and bask in the glorious light.

Our lives are a symphony, we'll write measures today
All things are possible when God conducts the stage.

Triggers

For we do not have a high priest who cannot sympathize with
our weaknesses, but One who has been tempted in all things
just as we are, yet without sin. Therefore let's approach the
throne of grace with confidence, so that we may receive mercy
and find grace for help at the time of our need.
Hebrews 4:15-16 NASB

Hey God.

Billboards are triggers. Also, the grocery store. Gas stations. TV shows, magazine ads, certain clothes I wear, glasses in the cupboard, lemons, salt, certain friends, certain times of the day. I want to be sober God but everything I see reminds me of my love affair with an addiction I unwillingly ended. I didn't want to give it up. It was killing me, stealing my life and the good things in it, and still I clung to it. Now like a bad breakup, I see reminders of my addiction everywhere I go. Hollow out my old memories and replace them with new life. May the triggers come fewer and farther in between. Give me strength to persevere when I feel Satan's claws dragging me backwards. *Amen.*

Dear God,

_____
_____
_____
_____
_____
_____
_____
_____
_____
_____
_____
_____
_____
_____
_____
_____
_____
_____
_____
_____

Evidence of the Answer:

_____
_____
_____
_____
_____

Prayer of Vigilance

But you, LORD, do not be far from me.
You are my strength; come quickly to help me.

Psalm 22:19 NIV

Dear God,

My thoughts are spiraling beyond my control. None of the tricks are working. The need to use is pounding against my skull. God, this is so hard, and I don't know what to do. I'm weak and I'm so afraid of falling, of letting everyone down, especially You. Distract me, God, please. Save me. Protect me. Just one night. The urge to succumb is always worse at night. Breathe in 2-3-4, out 2-3-4. In 2-3-4, out 2-3-4. You are with me in the darkness. Tonight, we will win. Sobriety is moment by victorious moment. I'm locking myself in my room. I don't need to make it through every night at once. I just need to be sober tonight. Tomorrow, help me to be courageous and vulnerable with people who want what's best for me. Help me to sleep soundly and wake up to sunshine on my face, with the triumphant feeling of victory. *Amen.*

Love,

Prodigal

Dear God,

_____
_____
_____
_____
_____
_____
_____
_____
_____
_____
_____
_____
_____
_____
_____
_____
_____
_____
_____

Evidence of the Answer:

_____
_____
_____
_____

Relapse

Be of sober spirit, be on the alert. Your adversary, the devil, prowls around like a roaring lion, seeking someone to devour. So resist him, firm in your faith, knowing that the same experiences of suffering are being accomplished by your brothers and sisters who are in the world.

1 Peter 5:8-9 NASB

Dear God,

I don't want to see it. I don't want to believe it. Prodigal has done so well lately. She's been sober for weeks. The signs are there and I want to close my eyes. Grant me courage to look at what's going on around me. Behaviors. Patterns. Words. Reveal Truth to me and give me the confidence to confront it. Where do we go from here? How can I approach the hard conversation with love when I am so, so hurt and scared—and angry? Help me put myself in Prodigal's shoes. How could this happen? Why? Prodigal can tell me. Is she ready to change? Help me to see that, too. I can't be her sobriety. That's not my job. Give me wisdom. Allow me to see You sitting across from her, talking with her and discussing what needs to happen next. Help me to step out of Your way so I can love her the way You do. *Amen.*

Dear God,

_____
_____
_____
_____
_____
_____
_____
_____
_____
_____
_____
_____
_____
_____
_____
_____
_____
_____

Evidence of the Answer:

_____
_____
_____
_____
_____

When an Addict Spirals

*Out of the depths I have cried to You, L*ORD*. Lord, hear my voice! Let Your ears be attentive To the sound of my pleadings. If You, L*ORD*, were to keep account of guilty deeds, Lord, who could stand? But there is forgiveness with You, So that You may be revered.*

*I wait for the L*ORD*, my soul waits, And I wait for His word. My soul waits in hope for the Lord More than the watch for the morning; Yes, more than the watch for the morning.*

Psalm 130:1-6 NASB

Lord Jesus,

I do not know what to do. This pain will not stop, and I cannot understand how to fix this. Lay with me in my pain Father. Wrap Your arms around me. Reach inside and heal the brokenness I cannot. Hold me in Your grace and give me peace Lord. I do not even have the words to cry out to you with, but You know every corner of my heart. You know what is broken. With outstretched hands I plead for Your presence and peace. Guide my heart because my way led to brokenness. I feel so alone in this darkness I have created. Tears of surrender stream down my face and my heart is peeled open. In Your mighty name I cry out for Your mercy to surround me. You are stronger than every demon I battle. May every chain be broken in Your name Jesus! Where I am weak I know You are strong Lord, I know Your love can heal it all. I want to resist the temptation, but I just spiral deeper and deeper into my addiction. I'm ensnared and can't escape. I need to rest in You, remember who I am, and to whom I belong. I pray this in the MIGHTY name of Jesus. *Amen.*

Dear God,

_____

_____

_____

_____

_____

_____

_____

_____

_____

_____

_____

_____

_____

_____

_____

_____

_____

_____

Evidence of the Answer:

_____

_____

_____

_____

Marriage Stress

In the same way, you who are younger, submit yourselves to your elders. All of you, clothe yourselves with humility toward one another, because,

"God opposes the proud but shows favor to the humble."

Humble yourselves, therefore, under God's mighty hand, that he may lift you up in due time. Cast all your anxiety on him because he cares for you.

1 Peter 5:5-7 NIV

Heavenly Father,

Thank you for knitting me together with my spouse. I love her dearly and am grateful for our partnership. The stress, though, of life, family, finances, work, and friends has bumped up the level of strain between us right now. Our family member's addiction adds its own frustrating layer. We're short with each other, pushy at times, selfish and self-centered other times. Please bring peace, that peace that passes all understanding, into our relationship.

Remind me, Father, to be patient, kind, land loving toward my partner. She isn't the cause of my anxiety and anger. I shouldn't take out my frustrations on her. I know I should cast all my fears and doubts at the foot of the cross. I do that now. Give all this to you, all my troubles, so that whatever irks me, I can let go. And focus on lowering the temperature of stress that has been stealing moments of laughter and love from me and my wife. Thank you, Lord. *Amen.*

Dear God,

_____
_____
_____
_____
_____
_____
_____
_____
_____
_____
_____
_____
_____
_____
_____
_____
_____
_____
_____

Evidence of the Answer:

_____
_____
_____
_____

The Children Involved

Start children off on the way they should go, and even when they are old they will not turn from it.

Proverbs 22:6 NIV

Dear God,

Embarrassment pounds against me. How will my children ever forgive me? What will the kids at their school say to them? Will they be bullied because of their deadbeat dad? Dear God please help me to be the parent you've called me to be. Be greater than my mistakes, and protect my children from my failings. Thank you for being their perfect loving Father who never fails them. Please show them how much they are loved. Protect them from following in my steps. Following you is the wisest choice they could ever make, and I pray that You would grow that desire in their hearts. Give them the strength and courage to pursue You, when the world tries to drag them away. *Amen.*

Dear God,

_____

_____

_____

_____

_____

_____

_____

_____

_____

_____

_____

_____

_____

_____

_____

_____

_____

_____

_____

Evidence of the Answer:

_____

_____

_____

_____

SOME PEOPLE CAN USE DRUGS and walk away. Not me. Addiction dug its claws in and imprisoned me. Any crack head will tell you, you'll spend your whole life "chasing that first high." That's usually their exact wording. Other users warned me. *They're exaggerating, surely.*

They weren't. Money ran out before drugs quenched the need. Crack addicts steal, but crack robs addicts blind, of money, sanity, reason, relationships, self-respect and freedom. Crack addicts despise who they become.

Urgency. Desperation. These are shadows of an addict's need. Most people need air to survive.

Imagine yourself thrown from a capsized sailboat and plunged into the sea. You fix your gaze on the sunlit outline of the sail rippling above you and claw to the surface. You're going to drown. Your lungs burn, desperate to inhale. You reach the sail. Fatigued arms press against nylon, but the sail is suctioned to the water. You clutch fistfuls of fabric and drag your body across the sail, hand-over-hand. Your lungs are on fire. You reach the mast and boost yourself upward. Your lips break the surface.

That breath. That first, life-reviving breath, is how addicts feel when they reach the high.

Many Christians judge addicts... "Why can't she sober up and take care of her kids?"

Pity them instead. Pray and fast for them. Thank God for the mercy He's shown you. Because you don't have to beg, borrow and steal for your oxygen. Your air is free.

Crack is a cannibal. In the throes of my addiction, I'd dissolved from 320 lbs. to 150 lbs. Bags beneath vacant eyes formed deep trenches. My skin paled to ashen as Satan's candy erased my existence. My outer appearance mirrored the Hollow consuming me. I escaped, only by the grace of God. If I ever smoked another rock, my wife and kids would never see me again.

Clint Evans, *The Prodigal's Son: Crackhead to Jesus Freak*

Legal Trouble

*I will be a father to him and he will be a son to Me;
when he does wrong, I will discipline him with a rod of
men and with strokes of sons of mankind, but My favor
shall not depart from him*

2 Samuel 7:14-15a NASB

Dear God,

Thank you for Prodigal's arrest last night. Thank you for saying, "Enough is enough," and putting a stop to the behavior that's been breaking Your heart. Thank you that for now, Prodigal has three hots and a cot, and is separated from the vice that's been killing him. Please make all addictive substances unavailable to Prodigal while he's in jail. Please grant him connections through the state/ county that will provide the help Prodigal needs to remain sober and clean, and make good choices. Show me my part in all the drama, especially if my place is backing away and creating distance, in order to allow You to move. Amen.

Dear God,

_____
_____
_____
_____
_____
_____
_____
_____
_____
_____
_____
_____
_____
_____
_____
_____
_____
_____
_____
_____

Evidence of the Answer:

_____
_____
_____
_____
_____

Sentenced to Jail

Because of the tender mercy of our God,
With which the Sunrise from on high will visit us,
To shine on those who sit in darkness and the shadow of death,
To guide our feet into the way of peace.
Luke 1:78-79 NASB

Dear God,

You've been in jail before. Throughout the ages, You sat in cells, sat in the dark, with those You love. And You love every incarcerated Prodigal. I believe this. I know this, so tonight I ask for You to bunk with Prodigal. Whisper in her ear that she is not alone, that You love her, that everything will be okay. Tell her that help is on the way, that You're in her corner. Help her to find rest and quiet in Your presence. Surround her with unexpected encouragement and hope in the darkest place. Dear God, please hold Prodigal tonight, and make her bed more warm and comfortable than it truly is, as she falls asleep in Your arms. *Amen.*

Dear God,

_____
_____
_____
_____
_____
_____
_____
_____
_____
_____
_____
_____
_____
_____
_____
_____
_____
_____
_____
_____

Evidence of the Answer:

_____
_____
_____
_____

An Addict Battling Depression

These things I have spoken to you so that in Me you
may have peace. In the world you have tribulation,
but take courage; I have overcome the world."

John 16:33 NASB

Mighty Father, Great Creator and Sustainer of Life,
I am oppressed. Afflicted by a formless darkness stretched over me
without end. I called to mind the beginning. A black, formless, and
shapeless void of darkness that stretched forth without beginning
or end. In the midst of this void, you recognize the need for your
presence, calling into being the wondrous and blazing light. With a
few words you spoke and breathed light into this darkness, forming
and shaping it with your hands. It's shown with rainbows of color, it's
sparkled with the luminance of your being. With it you brought life
and behold it was no longer void.

Father, step into this darkness with me. Breathe upon it and
bring forth life. Your presence sustains me and reminds me that I
am never ever alone. When the tempter offers darkness disguised
as light, help me see truth for what it is, Lord. A void that does not
sustain. Light the way for me with the comfort of your voice, like a
night light of peace in my darkest pain. Help me to step into the light,
to feel your stillness, staying with me when I feel alone. I want to see
you, to be bathed in the color of your beautiful light that will never
abandon or forsake me. Remind me of how far I've come. Comfort
me. I hear you whisper you will be with me until the end. *Amen.*

Dear God,

_____
_____
_____
_____
_____
_____
_____
_____
_____
_____
_____
_____
_____
_____
_____
_____
_____
_____
_____
_____

Evidence of the Answer:

_____
_____
_____
_____
_____

Suicidal Thoughts

Lord, my Rock, I call out to you for help.
Do not be deaf to me.
If you are silent,
I will be like those in the grave.
Hear the sound of my prayer,
when I cry out to you for help.
I raise my hands
toward your Most Holy Place.

Psalm 28:1-2 NCV

Dear God,

Shout louder than Legion in Prodigal's ear tonight. Legion chanting, taunting, spewing lies:

You're not worthy. The world would be better off without you. Your friends and family despise you. Just one moment, one choice, and all the pain goes away.

Shine light on these lies and expose them for what they are so Prodigal recognizes the truth.

Erase the lies and shout Your truth:

You are worthy of love and blessing. The world is better with you in it. You are loved. You are strong. You are a survivor. Your story matters. *Amen.*

Dear God,

_____
_____
_____
_____
_____
_____
_____
_____
_____
_____
_____
_____
_____
_____
_____
_____
_____
_____
_____

Evidence of the Answer:

_____
_____
_____
_____

"I love You, LORD, my strength." The LORD is my rock and my fortress and my savior, my God, my rock, in whom I take refuge; my shield and the horn of my salvation, my stronghold. I call upon the LORD, who is worthy to be praised, and I am saved from my enemies.

The ropes of death encompassed me, and the torrents of destruction terrified me. The ropes of Sheol surrounded me; the snares of death confronted me. In my distress I called upon the LORD, and cried to my God for help; He heard my voice from His temple, And my cry for help before Him came into His ears.

Psalm 18:1-6 NASB

Dear God,

What is the point of enrolling in treatment—again? Attending an AA meeting to get one more 24-hour chip? I could host a Bingo night for 70 seniors with all the chips I've collected. So many coins! So many promises to myself that I'm gonna get sober. So many attempts to do the right thing. And every single time, I fail. I'm in the same place I was years ago. And nothing has changed. I want to promise You that this time will be different. This will be the time I succeed. This will be the time that I stay clean. But we've been here before, too. I don't know why I bother. I've asked you for help in the past and I've still failed. I've begged You to take away my desire for the drug, but You never have. So what's left? What do I do now? I want to be clean. I envy people around me who can look at a bottle of alcohol and not want to drink. I envy people with prosperous jobs and put-together families. I want to be sober but I can't do it without Your help, God. I need you. And You know what I need more than I do. People, circumstances. Please pave the way for my success so that I can move on from this addiction and truly follow You into freedom. Please, God. *Amen.*

Dear God,

_____

_____

_____

_____

_____

_____

_____

_____

_____

_____

_____

_____

_____

_____

_____

_____

_____

Evidence of the Answer:

_____

_____

_____

_____

_____

Prayer Over the Presiding Judge

For by Him all things were created, both in the heavens and on earth, visible and invisible, whether thrones, or dominions, or rulers, or authorities—all things have been created through Him and for Him.

Colossians 1:16 NASB

God,

I can't believe Prodigal's choices have led us to a courtroom. Whose life is this? I've done the best I could for Prodigal, but right now I feel lost, like none of my efforts were good enough. Now I'm staring at the handcuffs on Prodigal's wrists, trying to figure out what choices led to this and where we go from here. And the judge at the front of the room, the one who holds Prodigal's fate, has boiled Prodigal's entire life down to a stack of paper. Please give the judge wisdom to truly see Prodigal. Help his decision to be what is best for everyone involved. Help me trust you with the outcome. May I see you moving in the courtroom today, God. Your will be done. Amen.

Dear God,

_____
_____
_____
_____
_____
_____
_____
_____
_____
_____
_____
_____
_____
_____
_____
_____
_____
_____
_____
_____

Evidence of the Answer:

_____
_____
_____
_____
_____

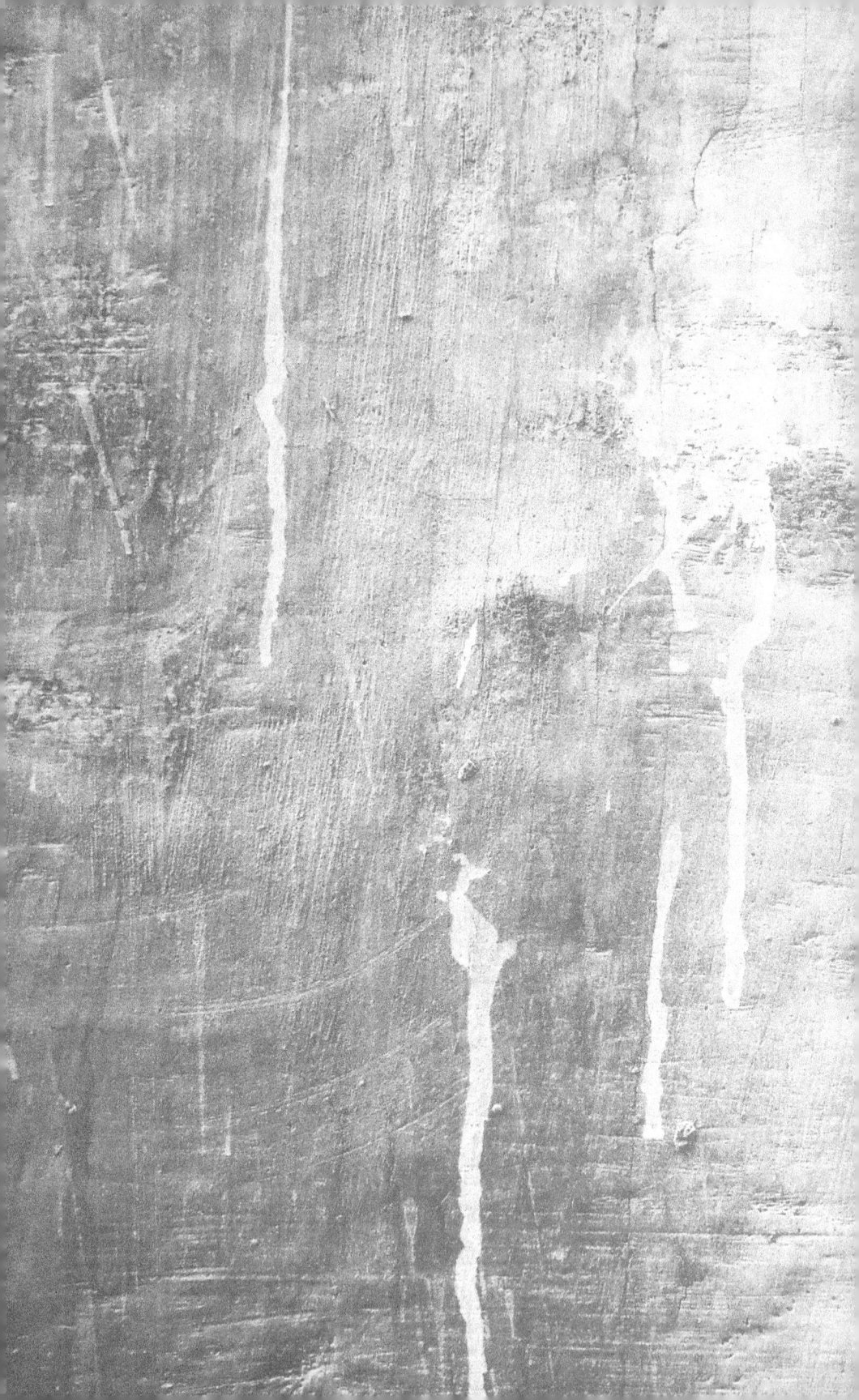

Listen,
Listen,
Listen

It don't matter how old they are,
Gotta start coachin' 'em young,
'Cuz there's a lot of bad voices out there
Tellin' kids they're worthless and unwanted.
That they ain't never gonna amount to nothin'.

Naw man.
Not my kids.
Not the ones God puts in front of me.

"Listen, listen, listen," I tell my son.
"I didn't always walk this way I'm walkin' now.
I didn't always walk this way.
It took me a long time to get here, man.
Believe that, yo.
What I'm tellin' you now,
Nobody told me then,
But I wish they did.

"So you pull your pants up,
Tie your tie.
And walk around dignified.
Respect feels different.
Listen, listen, listen."

Withdrawal

From inside the fish Jonah prayed to the LORD his God. He said:

*"In my distress I called to the LORD, and he answered me.
From deep in the realm of the dead I called for help, and you
listened to my cry. You hurled me into the depths, into the very
heart of the seas, and the currents swirled about me; all your
waves and breakers swept over me. I said, 'I have been banished
from your sight; yet I will look again toward your holy temple.'
The engulfing waters threatened me, the deep surrounded me;
seaweed was wrapped around my head. To the roots of the
mountains I sank down; the earth beneath barred me in forever.
But you, LORD my God, brought my life up from the pit.*

*"When my life was ebbing away, I remembered you, LORD,
and my prayer rose to you, to your holy temple.*

Jonah 2:1-7 NIV

Dear God,

Today is the day. It's time to kick this thing. I'm a few days in now and I feel like I'm being dragged down into a pit with chains clasped around my ankles, wrists, and neck. God help me! Pain is pricking my scalp. The battle is raging within me. I feel like the player in a combat video game, endlessly fighting. The war has depleted me to 0%. I'm on the verge of failure. One more blow and I'm down for the count. More fighting lies ahead of me, but I have no strength left. I feel weak and scatterbrained. Less than half of 1% of people successfully quit in opiate addiction, God. I want to be one of them. Please help me! I can't do this without you. Make it stop! Make it stop! Please douse the flames. Don't let me quit. I want to be free. *Amen.*

Dear God,

_____
_____
_____
_____
_____
_____
_____
_____
_____
_____
_____
_____
_____
_____
_____
_____
_____
_____
_____

Evidence of the Answer:

_____
_____
_____
_____
_____

Be gracious to me, God, according to Your faithfulness;
According to the greatness of Your compassion,
wipe out my wrongdoings.
Wash me thoroughly from my guilt
And cleanse me from my sin.
For I know my wrongdoings,
And my sin is constantly before me.
Against You, You only, I have sinned
And done what is evil in Your sight,
So that You are justified when You speak
And blameless when You judge.

Psalm 51:1-4 NASB

Dear God,

I'm dragging my demons to the surface kicking and screaming to face them head on. As I wake up from my addiction, emotional purge replaces the physical cleansing. The drug-induced cloud is clearing and I feel alive, but I'm waking up to the damage I've caused. I've been sobbing for days. Please God, forgive me for all the pain I've caused. Bring relief to my broken spirit. *Amen.*

Dear God,

_____

_____

_____

_____

_____

_____

_____

_____

_____

_____

_____

_____

_____

_____

_____

_____

_____

Evidence of the Answer:

_____

_____

_____

_____

So I find this law at work: Although I want to do good, evil is right there with me. For in my inner being I delight in God's law; but I see another law at work in me, waging war against the law of my mind and making me a prisoner of the law of sin at work within me. What a wretched man I am! Who will rescue me from this body that is subject to death? Thanks be to God, who delivers me through Jesus Christ our Lord!

Romans 7:21-25a NIV

Jesus,

This race is long and hard, a marathon that stretches mile after mile, kilometer after kilometer. My limbs ache, my back is strained, my mind urges me to stop, to lay down or take the easy road. I long to cast off this burden, to seek temporary relief instead of enduring step after step.

Yet, when I look over my shoulder, I see how far I've come—the mountains I climbed, the rocky trails I traversed. I see all the times I said "no" when I longed to say "yes." You supplied energy to my weary body, refreshment to my parched soul.

I have cast off the things that used to entangle me, that harmed me, that hurt those around me. If I ran on my own strength surely I would have given up on this race. But I have leaned on you. I allowed you to carry me when I wanted to quit. With each mile post I pass I am reminded this journey with you is worth the fight. Let this temptation pass for me. Provide a way for me to stand beneath the weight. Give me the wisdom to call out friends to help along the way. Strengthen me and my discernment, and help me to continue on, making the wisest decision on what path to take. Thank you Lord. You are here with me. Help me keep the faith, to run with endurance, to finish this race. *Amen.*

Dear God,

_____
_____
_____
_____
_____
_____
_____
_____
_____
_____
_____
_____
_____
_____
_____
_____
_____
_____

Evidence of the Answer:

_____
_____
_____
_____
_____

Hobbies and Self-care

The thief comes only to steal and kill and destroy; I came so that they would have life, and have it abundantly.
John 10:10 NASB

Dear God,

I never realized how many empty spaces I tried to fill with the drugs of my choice. Time, energy, money, My thoughts. There's so much more blessing to this life that I have missed out on because I was obsessed with getting high. Please continue to put new, exciting opportunities in my path to replace the former addiction, and to enjoy life in a new way. Please use these as opportunities for me to rebuild my relationship with you, and with others. Help me enjoy the world around me living out the full extent of my sobriety. Help me to live life to the fullest. Help me to treasure this time rather than mourning the minutes I lost. *Amen.*

Dear God,

_____
_____
_____
_____
_____
_____
_____
_____
_____
_____
_____
_____
_____
_____
_____
_____
_____
_____
_____

Evidence of the Answer:

_____
_____
_____
_____

Dreams of Using

No temptation has overtaken you except what is common to mankind. And God is faithful; he will not let you be tempted beyond what you can bear. But when you are tempted, he will also provide a way out so that you can endure it.

1 Corinthians 10:13 NIV

Dear God,

I pray against Prodigal's dreams of using, of Prodigal waking up in a panic with the taste on his tongue. The fear of failure, the jolt of adrenaline. Meet Prodigal in the tangled sheets. Extinguish Satan's attacks and guard the mind of Prodigal with the helmet of salvation. Remove the shadows, the memories of using and replace the nightmares with lightheartedness and peace. You alone Jesus, have the power to step into dreams while Prodigal sleeps. Jesus, Jesus, Jesus, please fight the battle for Prodigal beyond Prodigal's sight. *Amen.*

Dear God,

_____
_____
_____
_____
_____
_____
_____
_____
_____
_____
_____
_____
_____
_____
_____
_____
_____
_____
_____
_____

Evidence of the Answer:

_____
_____
_____
_____
_____

For our struggle is not against flesh and blood, but against the rulers, against the powers, against the world forces of this darkness, against the spiritual forces of wickedness in the heavenly places. Therefore, take up the full armor of God, so that you will be able to resist on the evil day, and having done everything, to stand firm.

Ephesians 6:12-13 NASB

Dear God,

Prodigal knows you. She hears you. She doesn't want to fall, doesn't want to fail, but the demons are crying out to her tonight. Prodigal has done so well lately. She'll be angry with herself for caving in. Please give her strength for right now, for this moment. Give Prodigal an inner power to step away and claim the victory. The doorbell, a phonecall, a thought. Break her concentration away from the addiction she's fixated on, and tonight, this one time, this one choice, help her to experience a victory. Sobriety happens one choice at a time, and only by Your strength. Infuse Prodigal with the desire to say, "no." Thank you that she is not alone tonight, but that You are with her. Amen.

Dear God,

_____
_____
_____
_____
_____
_____
_____
_____
_____
_____
_____
_____
_____
_____
_____
_____
_____
_____

Evidence of the Answer:

_____
_____
_____
_____
_____

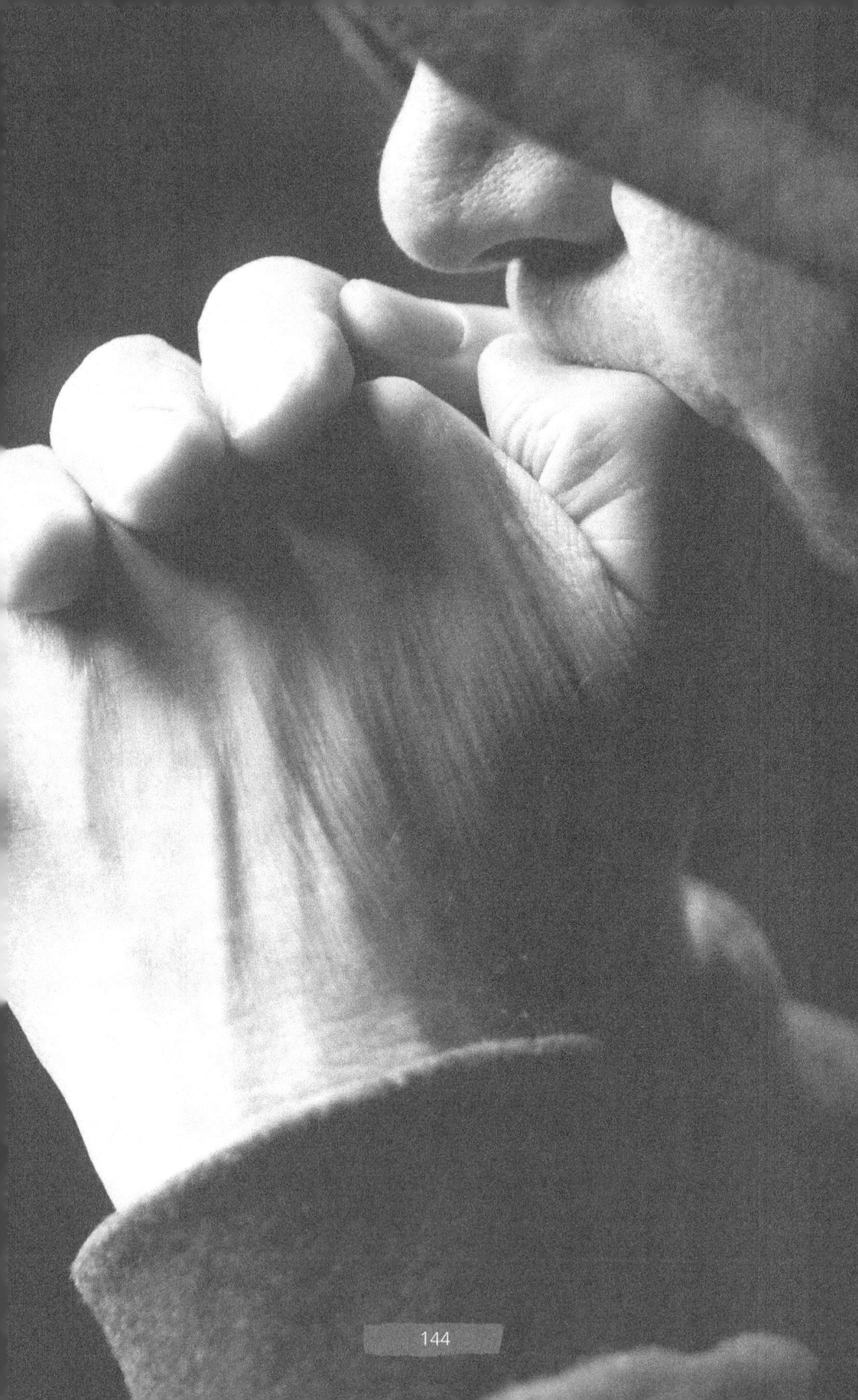

ADDICTS ONLY CONFESS when they want change and need help. "I don't think you were out of control," and "I don't think your problem is that bad," and "you can have just one," are the worst statements to say to a confessing addict. Those words grant the addict permission to return for seconds. And thirds. And in case you're reading this, and you disagree with me, you should know those statements were my addiction demon's favorites.

Clint Evans, *The Prodigal's Son: Crackhead to Jesus Freak*

A Fresh Start

*Therefore, if anyone is in Christ, the new creation has come:
The old has gone, the new is here! All this is from God, who
reconciled us to himself through Christ and gave us the ministry
of reconciliation: that God was reconciling the world to himself
in Christ, not counting people's sins against them. And he has
committed to us the message of reconciliation.*

2 Corinthians 5:17-18 NIV

Merciful Lord,

I praise you for the blessing of a new day. Of the chance to begin anew with you by my side. No matter what I have done, no matter what wrong I have chosen, your mercy is new each morning. You take the broken things and bind them, healing me and making me stronger. The things that once tore me to shreds can no longer penetrate the armor you've endowed me with. Where I once missed blessing an opportunity, with you I can fully take hold of the promise. In your holy name, I bind to the power of the enemy and declare that he will not win this war. Jesus, keep him from me in any way, creating a hedge around me so strong that not even one dart may pass through. Remind me, oh Lord, of the strength and power that does reside in me. Help me to take on this day and emerge victorious. *Amen.*

Dear God,

_____
_____
_____
_____
_____
_____
_____
_____
_____
_____
_____
_____
_____
_____
_____
_____
_____
_____

Evidence of the Answer:

_____
_____
_____
_____
_____

A Spirit of Power

For the Spirit God gave us does not make us timid,
but gives us power, love and self-discipline.
2 Timothy 1:7 NIV

Dear God,

Prodigal lives in fear. Fear of never getting sober, fear of what sobriety would look like. Fear of hurting others, fear of not getting high. Fear of facing past pain, fear of future hurts. Fear of being alone. Fear of what others will think. Please break the cycle of fear. Give prodigal strength to step out in faith. Allow room for healing to happen within prodigals battle scarred heart. Help prodigal feel loved, just as she is. Help her feel true acceptance from you and the people around her. May judgmental people fall away so that prodigal can receive the help she truly needs and known that her place is with you. *Amen.*

Dear God,

_____
_____
_____
_____
_____
_____
_____
_____
_____
_____
_____
_____
_____
_____
_____
_____
_____
_____
_____
_____

Evidence of the Answer:

_____
_____
_____
_____

When an Addict Truly Tries

This is the message we have heard from Him and announce to you, that God is Light, and in Him there is no darkness at all. If we say that we have fellowship with Him and yet walk in the darkness, we lie and do not practice the truth; but if we walk in the Light as He Himself is in the Light, we have fellowship with one another, and the blood of Jesus His Son cleanses us from all sin.

1 John 1:5-7 NASB

Father,

I know Prodigal's desire to stay clean. I see his determination to break the cycle in his life. I ask you to meet him where he is and to speak to his heart. Convict his spirit in a permanent way that he may find his way to You. May he desire to know you more. Walk with him hand in hand on his sobriety journey. Protect Prodigal against bad choices, and the desire to give up when he feels like a failure. Please guide his heart to stay on track. Heal the wounds of Prodigal's past and grant him freedom from the chains that hold him back. Help Prodigal to rest in Your love for him. May Prodigal no longer seek acceptance from others, as he grows in his confidence of his God-given identity. Protect him and guide him Jesus. *Amen.*

Dear God,

_____
_____
_____
_____
_____
_____
_____
_____
_____
_____
_____
_____
_____
_____
_____
_____
_____

Evidence of the Answer:

_____
_____
_____
_____

Future Possibilities

You also must obey the LORD—you must worship him with all your heart and remember the great things he has done for you.

1 Samuel 12:24 CEV

Heavenly Father,

I never dreamed I would make it this far. Yet here I am. Lord, I pray for your discernment as I take on new challenges and opportunities. Help me see where you need me. Please position me within your will. You gave me a high and holy call. Help me walk in obedience to your charge. I stand in a hallway of opportunities. Seal tightly doors not meant for me. Blow doors of prospect off their hinges. Give me courage as I go forth in this new possibility and remind me always of who I am in you. Amen.

Dear God,

_____

_____

_____

_____

_____

_____

_____

_____

_____

_____

_____

_____

_____

_____

_____

_____

_____

Evidence of the Answer:

_____

_____

_____

_____

_____

Education

And we know that God causes all things to work together for good to those who love God, to those who are called according to His purpose.

Romans 8:28 NASB

Dear God,

Prodigal is smarter than he gives himself credit for. And if You are for him, who can be against him? Endow Prodigal with confidence to step out in faith and enroll in school. He is so passionate and I believe education will help others see his capability the way I do. He has so much to offer this world, but he doubts himself. Pave the way with timing and finances so Prodigal's excuses fall to the ditch. Please pave the way for Prodigal's education. *Amen.*

Dear God,

_____

_____

_____

_____

_____

_____

_____

_____

_____

_____

_____

_____

_____

_____

_____

_____

_____

_____

Evidence of the Answer:

_____

_____

_____

_____

_____

Holding a Job

God, have You Yourself not rejected us?
And will You not go forth with our armies, God?
Give us help against the enemy,
For deliverance by man is worthless.
Through God we will do valiantly,
And it is He who will trample down our enemies.

Psalm 108:11-13 NASB

Dear God,

Prodigal's addiction is so all-consuming that now he can't even hold a job. What do we do now? We need money. I want to help him, but I can't. Any help I give now will only enable Prodigal to keep using. Please show Prodigal the futility of a life dictated by addiction. There's no way out. The drug is robbing Prodigal blind. Awaken Prodigal to the reachable possibilities with sober life. Create in Prodigal's heart, a desire to get clean. And please present him with opportunities for successful treatment. *Amen.*

Dear God,

_____
_____
_____
_____
_____
_____
_____
_____
_____
_____
_____
_____
_____
_____
_____
_____
_____

Evidence of the Answer:

_____
_____
_____
_____

The First
Country Christmas Song

VERSE 1

A melody beyond composition
A rising star, shepherds follow stage direction.
Angels amplify their declaration
With the first country Christmas song
The heavenly harmony causes hills to hum
Earth sings an anthem to her audience of one
Matt and Luke record a number 1
Rocks will roll with that country song.

CHORUS

Take me back to those country roads
Where kings' knees bend and everybody knows
A platinum album ain't got nothin' on a platinum sky.

Black sheep are welcome where the savior sleeps
And the prodigal God wandered from heaven's keep
To trade his throne for my cross and my death for his life.

God's first bed was a feeding trough
Because Grace says to Dirty, "You're Good Enough."
I don't deserve mercy, so Lord knows why.

VERSE 2

I turn off the headlights and pull in the drive
Peer at faces I recognize
Then I remove the key with a heave and a sigh
Turn off that country Christmas song.

"Oh, we didn't think you were coming."
Ma leans into Pop and whispers something
I turn my back and seconds later my truck is humming.
Tires peel as I turn on that Christmas song.

CHORUS
Take me back to those country roads
Where kings' knees bend and everybody knows
A platinum album ain't got nothin' on a platinum sky.

Black sheep are welcome where the savior sleeps
And the prodigal God wandered from heaven's keep
To trade his throne for my cross and my death for his life.

God's first bed was a feeding trough
Because Grace says to Dirty, "You're Good Enough."
I don't deserve mercy, so Lord knows why.

VERSE 3
Tires crunch gravel outside the nearest bar
It's amateur night so I grab my guitar
And the owner tells me there's an open hour
To sing a country Christmas song
Latches snap as I unclip the frayed, black case,
The room quiets down as I take my place.
Scootch the mike closer to my whiskered face
And bust out that country song . . .

CHORUS
Take me back to those country roads
Where kings' knees bend and everybody knows
A platinum album ain't got nothin' on a platinum sky.

Black sheep are welcome where the savior sleeps
And the prodigal God wandered from heaven's keep
To trade his throne for my cross and my death for his life.

God's first bed was a feeding trough
Because Grace says to Dirty, "You're Good Enough."
I don't deserve mercy, so Lord knows why.

VERSE 4

I'm scarred and filthy
And God still likes what he sees.
Lord Knows Why but in my heart I plead
Teach me your Christmas song.
God eyed my bloody knuckles and my jeans, all scuffed
Promised love to the least of us
Now I'm drinkin' water on the rocks instead of hops.
"Let me teach you this Good News Christmas Song."

CHORUS

Take me back to those country roads
Where kings' knees bend and everybody knows
A platinum album ain't got nothin' on a platinum sky.

Black sheep are welcome where the savior sleeps
And the prodigal God wandered from heaven's keep
To trade his throne for my cross and my death for his life.

God's first bed was a feeding trough
Because Grace says to Dirty, "You're Good Enough."
I don't deserve mercy, so Lord knows why.

VERSE 5

This sinner is tired of the same old song.
Please forgive me, Father, for what I've done.
I'm the lost Prodigal, searching for home,
I've hit a dead end on my own.
Too many burned bridges to remend
But at the back of the room, my dad walks in
With tears in his eyes for how things have been
Amazing Grace, that sweet, sweet song.

CHORUS

Take me back to those country roads
Where kings' knees bend and everybody knows
A platinum album ain't got nothin' on a platinum sky.

Black sheep are welcome where the savior sleeps
And the prodigal God wandered from heaven's keep
To trade his throne for my cross and my death for his life.

God's first bed was a feeding trough
Because Grace says to Dirty, "You're Good Enough."
I don't deserve mercy, so Lord knows why.

Show me your paths
and teach me to follow;
guide me by your truth
and instruct me.
You keep me safe,
and I always trust you.

You lead humble people
to do what is right
and to stay on your path.
In everything you do,
you are kind and faithful
to everyone who keeps
our agreement with you.

Psalm 25:4-5, 9-10 CEV

Dear God,

I come before You with a humble heart, seeking Your guidance and blessings. I ask for Your divine favor and wisdom as I strive for success in my endeavors. Please grant me the strength, determination, and clarity of mind to overcome any challenges that come my way. Help me to remain focused and diligent, and to always act with integrity and kindness. May Your light shine upon my path, leading me to achieve my goals and fulfill my purpose. I trust in Your infinite wisdom and grace, knowing that with Your support, all things are possible. *Amen.*

Dear God,

_____

_____

_____

_____

_____

_____

_____

_____

_____

_____

_____

_____

_____

_____

_____

_____

_____

_____

Evidence of the Answer:

_____

_____

_____

_____

_____

God's Favor

Even though I walk through the valley of the shadow of death,
I fear no evil, for You are with me;
Your rod and Your staff, they comfort me.
You prepare a table before me in the presence of my enemies;
You have anointed my head with oil;
My cup overflows.

Psalm 23:4-5 NASB

Lord,

I pray Your favor upon Prodigal. Be her battle cry and her rear guard. As she walks through the Valley of the Shadow of Death, light Prodigal's way and protect her from the assaults of the enemy. May angel armies surround her on all sides. May her weapon be Your words and Scriptural promises ringing in her ear. When Prodigal passes through danger unharmed, may hindsight reveal to Prodigal the undeniable proof of your presence. *Amen.*

Dear God,

_____
_____
_____
_____
_____
_____
_____
_____
_____
_____
_____
_____
_____
_____
_____
_____
_____
_____
_____

Evidence of the Answer:

_____
_____
_____
_____
_____

Positive Impact on the World

*In everything I showed you that by working hard in this
way you must help the weak and remember the words
of the Lord Jesus, that He Himself said, 'It is more
blessed to give than to receive.'*

Acts 20:35 NASB

Holy Spirit,

If I am ever to make a mark on this world, I pray it is one you would lead me toward. Let me never forget that I'm here because of the mercy of my Savior and filter all my plans through your will for me. I know that everything you have to teach me comes from the Son. Purify me, enrich my mind with the knowledge of the truth.

Guide my feet toward the path of obedience. Whatever my impact might be, let me be first and always submissive and obedient to you Lord. Place within me a discerning spirit that seeks to serve before it is served to love before it is loved, and understand before it is understood. Form me in the image of Jesus here on this earth. *Amen.*

Dear God,

_____
_____
_____
_____
_____
_____
_____
_____
_____
_____
_____
_____
_____
_____
_____
_____
_____
_____
_____

Evidence of the Answer:

_____
_____
_____
_____
_____

For I know the plans I have for you," declares the LORD,
"plans to prosper you and not to harm you, plans to give
you hope and a future. Then you will call on me and come
and pray to me, and I will listen to you. You will seek me
and find me when you seek me with all your heart.

Jeremiah 29:11-13a NIV

Jesus,

Help me not to despair. My tempter wants me to look at every circumstance around me, to the shifting tides, to the rain pelting me from every side. But you called to me from the midst of the storm. You are unafraid of it all, walking calmly upon the stormy sea. You call me to join you there, and do not rebuke the storm from raging. Jesus, give me courage to step onto the waves and walk toward you. Let me keep my eyes fixed on you and come in obedience toward your voice. I pray that you will still my throbbing heart, reminding me that you are with me, even when things don't go the way they should. Hold on to me, Blessed Savior. Where my grip on you would fail, hold me fast. Impart peace to my soul. Remind me that with you, there is no Plan B, only Plan A. Help me to remember you have a plan for me and my life. Keep worry from my mind. *Amen.*

Dear God,

Evidence of the Answer:

Friends Along the Journey

"Then the righteous will answer him, 'Lord, when did we see you hungry and feed you, or thirsty and give you something to drink? When did we see you a stranger and invite you in, or needing clothes and clothe you? When did we see you sick or in prison and go to visit you?'

"The King will reply, 'Truly I tell you, whatever you did for one of the least of these brothers and sisters of mine, you did for me.'

Matthew 25:37-40 NIV

Dear God,

I feel so helpless. I just want to take away Prodigal's pain. It is so hard to love her and watch her continue to make unhealthy decisions. I want to shake her and wake her up to reality, but this is her journey with You. God, speak to her heart. Show her that she is pushing away people who love her. Whatever her reasons for trying to keep us at arm's length, help Prodigal feel safe to be herself in our presence. Bring other people of strong character into Prodigal's life to walk alongside her, people who understand what she's going through, people she can trust. Give her loved ones strength to support her. I miss Prodigal more than I can say with words. Even if she is different, or if our relationship is different, I still yearn for a closeness with her again. *Amen.*

Dear God,

_____

_____

_____

_____

_____

_____

_____

_____

_____

_____

_____

_____

_____

_____

_____

_____

_____

_____

_____

_____

_____

Evidence of the Answer:

_____

_____

_____

_____

_____

I know that through your prayers and God's provision of the Spirit of Jesus Christ what has happened to me will turn out for my deliverance. I eagerly expect and hope that I will in no way be ashamed, but will have sufficient courage so that now as always Christ will be exalted in my body, whether by life or by death. For to me, to live is Christ and to die is gain.

Philippians 1:19-21 NIV

Dear God,

Please save Prodigal. While Prodigal is confined to this hospital bed, take advantage of your captive audience, currently detoxing against her will. Your healing Prodigal's body, thank you for that. Now I'm begging you, please heal her heart. Use this circumstance to awaken her spirit and show her how to have a dependency on you rather than the drug. You have to be stronger than the pull of her addiction, Jesus, because she'll never make it without you holding her on her path to sobriety. Lead her to a place of repentance and help her rely on you. *Amen.*

Dear God,

Evidence of the Answer:

DO YOU KNOW WHY repentant addicts make the most radical Jesus followers? Because they already know what losing life means. They know what slavery feels like. No place to lay your head? Check. Give up everything you own? Check. Nothing left to lose? Check. Despised by mother and father? Check. Check. Redeemed addicts understand grace more deeply than anyone else ever will.

Clint Evans, *The Prodigal's Son: Crackhead to Jesus Freak*

Why is life so hard?
Why do we suffer?
We are slaves in search of shade;
we are laborers longing
for our wages.
God has made my days drag on
and my nights miserable.
I pray for night to end,
but it stretches out
while I toss and turn.

Job 7:1-4 CEV

Dear God,

Anger, fear, and sadness, swirl around me. I thought you were protecting Prodigal! How could you let this happen? Don't you care? I'm devastated beyond recognition and I blame you. You could have stopped this. Where were you? Contempt exists where hope once resided. Resentment replaces joy. My faith is clinging by a thread. If you still love me, Jesus, you'll have to carry our relationship for now, because all my strength is gone. *Amen.*

Dear God,

_____
_____
_____
_____
_____
_____
_____
_____
_____
_____
_____
_____
_____
_____
_____
_____
_____
_____
_____

Evidence of the Answer:

_____
_____
_____
_____
_____

If Your Addict Passes Away

He died for us so that, whether we are awake or asleep,
we may live together with him.

1 Thessalonians 5:10 NIV

Well, God.

I guess you answered my prayers, huh? Prodigal is home. But heaven wasn't exactly the home I meant. A great, big hole replaced the chaos Prodigal once filled. I feel like a cannon just shot through my center. Part of me died with Prodigal. And I'm not sure I'll ever recover. Can you tell me my future? Does this pain get easier?

As hard as this is to say, thank you for Prodigal, and the time we shared. Thank you for giving Prodigal rest from depression and from the exhausting battle to remain sober. Tell Prodigal I say hi, and to save a seat for me, until we meet again. *Amen.*

Dear God,

_____

_____

_____

_____

_____

_____

_____

_____

_____

_____

_____

_____

_____

_____

_____

_____

_____

Evidence of the Answer:

_____

_____

_____

_____

_____

Salvation

He himself bore our sins in his body on the cross,
so that we might die to sins and live for righteousness;
"by his wounds you have been healed." For "you were
like sheep going astray," but now you have returned
to the Shepherd and Overseer of your souls.

1 Peter 2:24-25 NIV

Dear God,

Prodigal can't believe in you unless she sees you. She won't understand your goodness unless you reveal yourself to her. She has to accept the free gift that You offer, but first she has to know the gift is there for the taking. Make Yourself real to Prodigal, undeniably present. Tear down her walls and the barriers she's put between herself and You. Open her eyes. Help her to see. She's tried doing this life thing without you, and it's not working. And how could it? So, give her You. Bring her to the threshold of salvation, and give her the courage to cross over from unbelief into faith. *Amen.*

Dear God,

_____
_____
_____
_____
_____
_____
_____
_____
_____
_____
_____
_____
_____
_____
_____
_____
_____
_____
_____
_____
_____

Evidence of the Answer:

_____
_____
_____
_____

Celtic Blessing

Then young women will dance and be glad,
young men and old as well.
I will turn their mourning into gladness;
I will give them comfort and joy instead of sorrow.
I will satisfy the priests with abundance,
and my people will be filled with my bounty,"
declares the LORD.

Jeremiah 31:13-14 NIV

A Celtic Blessing

May the road rise to meet you,
May the wind be always at your back.
May the sun shine warm upon your face,
The rains fall soft upon your fields.
And until we meet again,
May God hold you in the palm of his hand.

Dear God,

_____
_____
_____
_____
_____
_____
_____
_____
_____
_____
_____
_____
_____
_____
_____
_____
_____
_____
_____

Evidence of the Answer:

_____
_____
_____
_____

Tell the world what you think with a review!

The Best Way to Say "Thank You."

 Did you appreciate this prayer journal? Reviews are currency with Amazon. The more reviews a book acquires, the more visibility the title receives. Especially with independently published works, the numbers matter. The best way to thank your favorite authors is by leaving reviews.

Join the Newsletter to Receive Three Free Chapters of
The Prodigal's Son: Crackhead to Jesus Freak

COMING SOON

AT 1:30 A.M. SAMANTHA EVANS received the phone call every spouse dreads. "Mrs. Evans, this is Sergeant Reid with the police department. There's been an accident." Six hours later, she received another call. "Mrs. Evans, I'm calling from the hospital. We found something on the CT scan."

Instead of preaching that Sunday, Pastor Clint Evans went to jail with a BAC of .24, a cancer diagnosis, and a felony charge of fleeing police. The Prodigal's Son: Crackhead to Jesus Freak chronicles a Christian's lifelong battle against demons, addictions, and unworthiness. This story portrays God's backlash of grace toward a man whom others branded "unredeemable."

The Prodigal's Son flings church doors open wide to the world's ragamuffins and challenges pew-squater saints to stop measuring their godly perfection against the dirty, homeless and addicted. From gutter to pulpit to ditch to grace to grave, The Prodigal's Son speaks volumes of a God who crawls into the darkest corners of humanity and redeems those who believe they aren't worth saving.

Sam Evans Tschritter

Author of prayers on pages: 2, 10, 18, 28, 36, 42, 50, 52, 54, 60, 64, 70, 78, 80, 82, 88, 100, 106, 108, 114, 118, 120, 124, 126, 128, 132, 134, 138, 140, 142, 148, 154, 156, 164, 172, 176, 178

Multi-award-winning author S. E. Tschritter (pronounced Shredder) specializes in articulating grief and loss, leading grievers toward hope and healing. Whether poetry, fiction, or non-fiction, Tschritter writes content that will stick with readers long after they close the cover. Her 20-plus years of leadership experience and contributions to over 30 books enable her to serve others, speaking truth with transparency, humor, and love.

Tschritter grew up in Chicagoland and has also lived in Minnesota and Oregon, granting her widespread views of people all over the country. She currently resides in Simpsonville, South Carolina with her husband, their three teen and preteen daughters, cats named Pitter and Patter, and their Siberian husky whom she lost the vote to name Onomatopoeia. Nothing refreshes Tschritter's soul like gardening. She gardens to work through plot holes, writer's block, character development, and book ideas. Tschritter spends a great deal of time gardening.

Ashley Worrell

Second chances describes author Ashley Worrell and her characters. Ashley is a recovering HR executive, an army wife and an umpteenth-generation Appalachian. She currently resides in South Carolina with her husband and their two sons and daughter. Her book Radiance of the Moon finaled in the ACFW Genesis contest. Read about her characters or find out more at ByAshleyWorrell.com.

The Hebridean Shield Series Books 1-3
Available on Amazon Now.

AMONG HECTOR'S FIGHTERS, Calum MacLean is the most savage. Able to strike with lightning-fast precision, Calum's upbringing on the tribal island of Jura has secured his place as one of the Isles' most gifted warriors. Yet it is his heathen past he desires to outrun most, having fled his home after betraying his father, and his duty as tànaiste. But when his secret role in the Shield is exposed by a bard called the Storyteller, Calum is forced to return to the island he escaped from.

Ten years after the ill-fated decision that cost her everything, Freya MacSorley is trapped in a double life. With her father she lives in extreme seclusion, and in secret, she spins tales and songs about the lad she helped escape, and the missions he carries out as a member of the revered Shield. Assured that they will never meet again, Freya is stunned when Calum returns to the shores of Jura—no longer a lad, but a fierce and deadly warrior, one that is on a mission to find the bard who has betrayed him.

When Freya is harmed and Jura attacked, Calum is faced with a series of life-altering decisions. Instead of fleeing from heathen Jura, he begs God to send him on his most important mission—to protect the bride he is beginning to cherish and to save his homeland. As the threats to Freya's life grow more brazen, Calum begins to realize that all is not as he believes.

Other Books By S.E. Tschritter

Do you feel helpless, watching a loved one grieve a loss that you can't fathom? Written by a griever, these books reach the heart of someone in grief. Give the gift of words when you can't muster them yourself.

Someone grieving a loss will find themselves saying, "Yes, this" when they read, and ruminating on the words long after they close the cover. "When I leave this earth, that's what I want people to whisper about me in my absence—'She told them they were loved.'"

~S. E. Tschritter

Unique Features Include:
• The journaler becomes the author of his/ her story
• Designed by a mom of three heaven-born babies
• Journal prompts listed in the table of contents
• Thoughtful gift for grieving mothers • Captivating photos • Coloring pages • Open-ended journal space
• Excerpt from *Love Letters to Miscarriage Moms*
• Encouraging Quotes • Bible Verses

In this book, over 40 men and women lend vulnerable insight into their experiences with infant loss. With raw honesty, Sam shares hard-won lessons learned during her darkest days. From practical suggestions to spiritual encouragement, *Love Letters to Miscarriage Moms:* Validates unique grief experiences, provides ideas for self-care and healthy coping strategies, and lays bare legitimate, complex spiritual doubts.

2023 Golden Scroll Award, Advanced Writers and Speakers Association
2023 International Book Awards, Finalist, Health: Women's Health
2023 International Book Awards, Finalist, Best Interior Design
2010 Orange County Christian Writers Conference Award

Larry J. Leech II

Author of prayers on pages: 38, 96, 112

Larry J. Leech II first came to know Christ as a young child. He knows all about second chances. Third chances. Thousandth chances. More than forty years ago, Larry started his career as a sportswriter in southwestern Pennsylvania where he covered prep sports, college sports, and the Pittsburgh Pirates and Steelers. In 2004, after 2,300 published articles, Larry shifted to book publishing. For twenty-plus years he has ghostwritten thirty-four books, edited more than 500 manuscripts, and coached hundreds of authors through the writing and publication process. Larry is the writing coach and editor of award-winning authors, as well as Acquisitions Editor and Master Book Coach at Illumify Media. He lives in Upstate South Carolina with wife. His favorite villain of all-time is Darth Vader and he incorporates Star Wars references into his teaching at every opportunity. Subscribe to his Youtube channel @Manuscript_Medic for free tips on how to share your own story or learn more on his website: LarryLeech.com.

  @Manuscript_Medic

Erin Niebuhr Hernandez

Author of prayers on pages: 4, 8, 20, 22,
24, 46, 48, 62, 94, 110, 150, 170

Nearly fifteen years beyond the darkness of addiction, Erin volunteers at her local church and shares her testimony of grace in the surrounding area. She lives in Southern Minnesota with her husband Jaime, their two daughters, and their Dalmatian, Ace. Together, Jaime and Erin run their business Top Hat Candle. Each candle is crafted by hand and created with scents that evoke a sense of warmth and nostalgia. Visit their website at https://tophatcandleco.com/

tophatcandleco.com

Kelly Evans

Author of prayers on pages: 56, 90, 162

Kelly is a 13-year-old who believes in the power of prayer and its ability to connect people. She wrote these prayers with her heart, inspired by her passion to help others find peace and encouragement. When she's not writing, she enjoys playing viola, drawing, reading her Bible, figure skating, and proving her Mom wrong.

Thy word is a lamp unto my feet, and a light unto my path.
Psalm 119:105 KJV